FREE STUFF
Guide for Everyone

Free and Good Deals That Save You Lots of Money

Peter Sander

Humanix Books

Free Stuff Guide for Everyone

Humanix Books, P.O. Box 20989, West Palm Beach, FL 33416, USA
www.humanixbooks.com | info@humanixbooks.com

Library of Congress Cataloging-in-Publication Data

Names: Sander, Peter J., author.
Title: Free stuff guide for everyone : free and good deals that save you lots of money / Peter Sander.
Description: West Palm Beach, FL : Humanix Books, 2017. | Includes index.
Identifiers: LCCN 2016051806 (print) | LCCN 2017007335 (ebook) | ISBN 9781630060763 (paperback) | ISBN 9781630060770 (Ebook)
Subjects: LCSH: Free material. | Consumer education. | Special sales. | Cash discounts. | Deals. | Home economics. | BISAC: REFERENCE / Consumer Guides.
Classification: LCC AG600 .S26 2017 (print) | LCC AG600 (ebook) | DDC 658.8/2—dc23
LC record available at https://lccn.loc.gov/2016051806

Interior Design: Scribe Inc.

Disclaimer: The information presented in this book is meant to be used for general resource purposes only; it is not intended as specific financial advice for any individual and should not substitute financial advice from a finance professional.

ISBN: 978-1-63006-076-3 (Trade Paper)
ISBN: 978-1-63006-077-0 (E-book)

Printed in the United States of America
10 9 8 7 6 5 4 3 2 1

Free Stuff is dedicated to all you "seekers" out there, who, like me, experience some visceral pleasure, as well as tangible savings, out of tracking down a good deal.

You know who you are.

Table of Contents

Acknowledgments

I would like to recognize my late parents, Jerry and Betty Sander, and my extended family for their constant "drip" of their frugal and sensible ways into my psyche. I would also like to thank my friends and sons Julian and Jonathan, who have been known on occasion to tease me about my frugal ways, for thus (and quite inadvertently) embellishing my motivation to do this project. Finally I'd like to thank the team at Humanix Books, most particularly Mary Glenn and Deb Englander, for giving me this opportunity to compile these money-saving techniques and experiences into a book.

Introduction

"Free!"

"Deal!"

"Discount!"

You hear the words everywhere. You see the signs everywhere. They're all over the Internet.

As a consumer, don't these three words perk your ears up? Make you want to hear more?

These three words are the power appetizers of commerce.

They get your attention. More important, they are harbingers of a "win-win" that makes our daily commercial world go round. They bring together you, Mr. or Ms. Consumer, with "them"—Mr. or Ms. Marketer.

The Deals Are Everywhere

I just turned 60. Guess what? I get 10 percent off any meal at Chick-fil-A. I can get a free drink at any KFC. I can get 15 percent off at Kohl's every Wednesday. I can get 30 percent off movie tickets at AMC Theaters (and 60 percent on Tuesdays). Heck, if I had joined AARP, which I could have done at age fifty, I would have gotten 15 percent off any meal at Outback Steakhouse.

And that just scratches the surface. I can be any age and get 10 percent off most hotel rooms in the country with an American Automobile Association (AAA) membership. If I book in advance, I can get 20 percent or even 30 percent off! I can get free or very cheap dental or eye or hair care if I live close to a professional school and free museum days almost anywhere. And I can get a free battery check and install at almost any auto parts retailer and free string cheese samples and who knows what else at one of the many "free stuff" portals I'll describe later!

And if I'm active or retired military or a veteran, I can get discounts everywhere, from free admission to national parks to a 10 percent discount at Lowe's. If I'm a student, I can get $150 off many major computer purchases and discount museum admissions; if I'm a teacher, I can get 20 percent off at Barnes & Noble.

Why So Many Deals?

First, there's you. You're looking to save money, to make your precious dollars stretch a little further, or even to get stuff for free (yes, there's a lot out there). You live on a budget. Or some of you just crave the sheer satisfaction of the "win" itself—that is, getting a good deal on something.

Then there's a marketer, someone responsible for selling more of a product or a service. It may be a business owner, an employee, or even a "hired gun" in an agency hired to, one way or another, stimulate sales of a product or service.

They do this by gaining your attention. They can gain your attention by boasting about the product with advertising. But most of us have learned to tune out those ads, right? What speaks to us—those of you who bought this book, anyhow—is *price*. Give me a good deal, and now I'm interested. Is that you?

If it is, we have the win-win. The marketer wins by *giving* you a good deal; you win by *getting* that good deal.

This book is about finding that win-win.

Becoming a Proactive Seeker

But this book is also about making you a proactive seeker, not a responder, to such offers. Why is that important? Because if we can be proactive—learn *where and how to seek* freebies, deals, and discounts—we'll end up getting these deals on *things we want or need.*

If we're merely responders, you know what happens. We leave ourselves at the feet of the marketers. We buy stuff we don't want or need just because of the deal. Yuck!

Becoming a *skilled* proactive seeker is also a big part of what *Free Stuff Guide for Everyone: Free and Good Deals That Save You Lots of Money* is all about.

More Important than Ever

And knowing your way around the world of deals is more important than ever. Why?

Because the world of deals has expanded in a huge way. There are so many of them—too many to know about and too many to find, especially if you're looking for a good deal on a particular item—it can be like a needle in a haystack exercise.

We all leave money on the table every day. With virtually anything you buy, there's a deal somewhere. There's a marketer who wants to increase sales, and that marketer knows that there are a lot of "you" out there.

This book is designed to help you through that haystack: one, to know what's in it; two, to find your way to the deal; and three, to have some fun in the search.

Fish vs. How to Fish

Free Stuff Guide for Everyone cannot be an all-inclusive guide to all the freebies, deals, and discounts out there. Why? It's simple. There are too many—millions. And they change. "Twenty percent off, good till October 31." How do I capture that and publish it in a book that takes months to put together and is designed to be useful for years? I can't.

Bill Clinton once described U.S. foreign policy as "power by example, not examples of power." I'm going to borrow part of that prescient phrase for a minute to describe this book. While I do list hundreds of actual freebies, deals, and discounts in the pages that follow, my real intent is to give you "power by example"—to "teach you how to fish" by giving examples of what you'll find and where to look.

I can't give you all the freebies, deals, and discounts. But I can make you better at finding them. I can teach you *how* to fish, and to extend the cliché, I can teach you *where* to fish.

Who Am I to Write This?

Good question.

I write a book about investing called *The 100 Best Stocks to Buy* (Adams Media, published annually). I don't make a lot of money writing the book, but I do pretty well following my own investment advice. Similarly, with this book I hardly made enough to retire, but I have supplemented my "net" income considerably by learning more about where and how to shop! And my status as a "cusp" senior at age 60 now also helps to unlock the best deals on stuff.

As a researcher and author, I consider myself an expert on finding value. I find value in stocks as mentioned above. I find value in personal finances with *Free Stuff Guide for Everyone: Free and*

Good Deals That Save You Lots of Money, and others. In the mid-2000s, I found value in places to live with my *Cities Ranked & Rated* series. While I was still in the corporate world, I found value in customers as customer valuation manager for a large Fortune 500 tech company.

Of course, I still believe part of the path to financial success is to *not buy* a lot of stuff—but when you do, do it right! That said, I'm not just talking about "stuff"—a good bit of what you'll find here is devoted to services and to experiences like travel, entertainment, culture, dining out, and the many pleasures in life you can earn and enjoy.

It's all about finding value—the central theme of this book.

The Journey to Freebies, Deals, and Discounts

Enough about me. Enough about this book, what it is and what it isn't.

Allow me to give you a glimpse of what you're about to see. I don't intend that you read *Free Stuff Guide for Everyone* from cover to cover. You can if you want. I do recommend reading Part I, then using what follows on an as-needed and as-curious basis. Over time, you'll become a smarter, savvier, and cleverer shopper. You'll decide where you want to fish and what gear you want to use.

Part I, "Freebies, Deals, and Discounts: A Thought Process" gives you a clear-eyed view of what to expect with Chapter 1, "The Art of the Deal," and then a trip through my favorite ways to find deals, mostly online and through groups and organizations like AAA and AARP. By the time you finish Part I, you'll be set up to fish; it's just a matter of picking a day, deciding what you're looking for, and casting your line into the water.

From there, I divide the water into two "ponds"—the first being the necessities in life like food; clothing; shelter; automotive services; and professional services, such as health care; and legal and financial services. The second "pond" is the "wants"—the pleasurable things like eating out, travel, recreation, and other "discretionary" items. You'll find plenty of deals in both ponds; there are twelve chapters of examples between them.

For some of you, deal finding will become a daily habit and part of your morning routine. For others, you'll do it when you're looking for something specific.

Either way, you'll become a happier, wealthier, and more successful shopper. And for most of you, when the freebies and deals are a bitin', you'll be having fun!

Part I

Freebies, Deals, and Discounts

A Thought Process

CHAPTER 1

The Art of the Deal

What You Need to Know about Today's Freebies, Deals, and Discounts

Thinking of having a nice steak dinner at Outback Steakhouse? I think about it all the time. But now I know a secret: there are almost always a few offers available to take some of the sting out of the cost of dinner. Fifteen percent off if you're an AARP member? A coupon for $5 off for a dinner for two if you aren't? These deals, by themselves, won't make you rich. But by the time you experience such savings a dozen or even a hundred times annually across your shopping and entertaining universe, it becomes very real money indeed.

And you can do it all with the convenience of your computer, or for those born after 1982, your mobile device.

Deals, discounts, coupons, freebies. They're everywhere. Thousands of them. An *explosion* of them! By the time you finish reading this book, you won't go anywhere or shop for anything without first checking the deals that might be available. These days, it's easy!

Eager marketers are hawking the wares of eager businesses and organizations ever more aggressively. Numbed by regular advertising, their audience—you and me—is responding more and more to deals. Too, the recent Great Recession taught us all to cut back a little—to become more frugal. And now the Internet provides a better-than-ever electronic path to connect marketers with all of us.

Hundreds of companies, some big enough to have publicly traded shares, act almost as "exchanges" to bring all those deals our way! It's pretty exciting, and both habitual and casual deal seekers can find good deals in seconds—or spend hours perusing the deal landscape on any given day.

And many do.

In this chapter, I'll give an overview of the ins and outs of free stuff, deals, and discounts.

The World of Free

It's *free*. Woohoo!

Among a sea of pretty catchy four letter words, behaviorists and marketers have found that the word "free" generates one of the strongest responses—a *favorable* response—of all the words we commonly use. Neuromarketing specialist Roger Dooley, in his article "The Power of FREE," states that "a preference for 'free' seems to be [a] feature hardwired into our brains." So I thought reviewing free stuff—"freebies"—would be a good way to start off this chapter and book.

Freebies: Too Good to Be True?

Free? Really? You're skeptical. It's understandable.

Knowing what we all know about business and capitalism, it sort of defies common sense for companies or organizations to give us stuff for free. Businesses that sell product or services, after all, are in business to earn money, right? How can they earn money if they get no money in exchange for offering you their product?

It's a good question—giving stuff away for free goes against our common sense notion of what business and capitalism are all about. But that said, there are "free" offers everywhere. There are entire websites devoted to identifying and connecting you with free products and services. I'll examine five of them in the next chapter.

Strings Attached, Are There?

These are good questions to ask: *How* free? *Why* free? How and why does a business or organization give stuff away for free? If you understand how and why you'll become a better freebie shopper—not only will you find more freebies but you'll also get to know the abundant "catches" and pitfalls of the freebie world.

The biggest catch, really, is that "free" usually isn't really free. In most cases, providers of free items want something in return for their offer. That "something" isn't money—but it very often is information about you or even a *relationship* with you. That information, and especially the relationship, can be used to learn more about you and to market more stuff to you.

So be careful out there. Your acceptance of an offer for $2 worth of free string cheese may result in a benign and even autonomous information grab—"someone living in zip code 12345 likes string cheese."

But more often than not, especially on the Internet, you'll be asked for an e-mail address. Your "free" string cheese may result in your getting spam e-mail, sometimes not just from whoever gave you the string cheese. You'll get a cookie on your computer, paving the way for ads and other contacts from that company and possibly other companies in the food business. You may be asked to—or required to—complete a survey. You'll be known to the world as someone who likes string cheese. To marketers of string cheese, such information is golden.

And watch out—you may get dinged for shipping and handling charges, which can exceed the value of the string cheese.

Of course, there are other catches. People will brag about getting into a concert for "free" by being an usher or for volunteering in their medical booth. Sure, they didn't pay money—but they paid in work, in transportation costs, and in being distracted during the show! If you give up something to get something, it isn't really free. But it still may be worth it—I don't discourage you from volunteering to usher the next Doobie Brothers concert!

And of course I don't discourage you from seeking freebies in the first place—the savings can add up, you can learn a lot too, and it's fun.

But—as with most things that can look too good to be true—*caveat freebie*!

What about Loyalty Programs?

Loyalty programs, like airline or hotel points programs, offer lots of valuable "free" stuff, such as free flights, first class upgrades, free rooms, and so forth. But are these really "free?" Generally not—you have to buy enough flights or rooms or earn points elsewhere to acquire enough points for the "free" offer.

Buy four or five flights, and you may get enough points for a free flight, depending on the program, what flights you buy, and what flight you try to get for free. So the "free" flight amounts to more of a post-event discount or a rebate for other flights you've taken.

Furthermore, loyalty programs are among the higher forms of "relationships" a business will establish with a customer. They become a major conduit for more marketing promotions and offers—so rather than being "free" you've opened up another channel for what can be a deluge of marketing contacts.

I don't think this qualifies as "free." Further, I am not going to cover loyalty programs in this book, as they are pretty well understood by most people and differ only subtly from one program to the next. That's not a surprise, as a handful of agencies run most of the loyalty for the companies who have them. Further, as each company tries to stay competitive, there's a tendency for each to match each other's loyalty program benefits.

Freebies Come in Many Flavors

With the caveats on the table and loyalty programs excluded from what I truly consider free, there is still a lot of free stuff out there. When you get right down to it, the list is surprisingly long.

- *True freebies.* Sometimes companies simply give away free stuff, mainly to extend their brand or complement something that they sell. Software is a good example—Adobe has never charged for its Acrobat Reader software because they want to extend their brand and become a de facto standard for document and image handling and printing. Google and

Apple have free versions of word processing and spreadsheet programs. Heck, most of the Internet is free!

- *Free samples.* Far more widespread is the availability of free samples. Entire websites are designed around connecting you with free samples (see next chapter). Try our macaroni and cheese for free! Of course, they're hoping you like it, and you are willing to buy from here to time eternal. Free samples are ubiquitous but tend to be small and often require you to supply contact info and possibly take a survey.
- *Free trials.* Free trials are like free samples but may be for an ongoing test market and may involve much higher valued items like pharmaceuticals.
- *Birthday freebies.* It's become a tradition (in the United States anyway) for companies to offer anything from a free meal or chocolate fudge sundae to a healthy 15 to 20 percent discount on one's birthday! Of course, the idea is to get you to come back when it's *not* your birthday!
- *National day freebies.* Similar to birthdays, you can get a free donut from Dunkin' Donuts on National Doughnut Day, and Sonic sells hot dogs for a buck on National Hot Dog Day. To track what "day" it is, check out nationaldaycalendar.com or subscribe to their daily newsletter—it tells you what day it is but not necessarily what's free—but it's fun anyhow. Some companies have their own special days, like Ben & Jerry's Free Cone Day. You'll just have to search the bushes of the Internet for some of your favorite freebies!
- *Free with purchases.* Buy a new camera and get a camera bag for free! This is very common and is really just a way to get a modest discount on buying the product.

- *"BOGO."* Buy one, get one of equal or lesser value. Not "free" but amounts to a discount of as much as 50 percent on the first one you buy. Good sale, but make sure you need two of whatever it is, and watch out for other strings attached.
- *Free service.* Far more often overlooked are scenarios where a service is offered for free. It can be maintenance on a big ticket item you buy (not really free) or an offer to get your brakes checked (which may not be free either if the service provider is biased to recommend a brake job you might not need). Watch out for free or heavily discounted heating and air conditioning service—been burned on this one personally—the "free" or discounted offer just gets them onto your property to sell, sell, sell. Still, aside from these negatives, many free service offers, such as Les Schwab fixing tires for free even if you don't own their tires, are simply gestures of goodwill and brand building designed to motivate you to buy there next time—and why not?
- *Free shipping.* Also often overlooked are free shipping offers—which can really add up for large items you'd have to wrestle home yourself, such as furniture or large electronics.
- *Just plain free.* People just needing to get rid of extra stuff (and don't we all have a lot?) will put it out on their lawn with a "free" sign on it. But that isn't a very efficient way to find it, is it? A more efficient way is through the "free" page in the Craigslist "for sale" section.

It's a long list, and when you're dealing with businesses, there's a win-win in there somewhere so there can be a lot of catches. But with some care, you can make lots of good freebie deals over time.

Saving Big with Deals and Discounts

This book will connect you with freebies. But freebies, as discussed above, tend to be small and often not really free. The real money to be "made"—saved—over time tends to be in the form of deals and discounts. Thus deals and discounts cannot be ignored and will necessarily become a big part of this book. So for every category for which I identify freebies, I will also highlight deals and discounts.

Not Free—but a Darned Good Deal

I believe that nobody should ever pay full price for anything.

Now there are some exceptions—such as last minute travel and health care—where the seller has all the cards, so to speak, and can afford to say, "take it or leave it."

With these unfortunate exceptions in mind, I stand by my statement.

Why? Because, as I mentioned at the outset, businesses are eager to make the sale. They want you in their (virtual or actual) store. They want to establish a relationship with you. They want to find out more about you. And there's a lot of competition out there.

This anxiety drives them to make offers to get your attention. Price offers have become more effective over time as we've become more frugal and have learned to tune out advertising—you can tune out an ad, but can you tune out a deal? Deals get more attention than regular ads, no? For most of us, anyway.

So there are deals everywhere. Special discounts and offers, which once filled your newspaper and mailbox, now fill the Internet. The advent of the Internet and its various ways to deliver discount offers has expanded the potential to connect offers with customers exponentially, and marketers haven't been blind to the opportunity.

It's fair to ask—if consumers are sensitive to price, why don't companies just lower their prices? If companies lowered the price on everything, they'd lose revenue across the board. By offering deals and discounts, only the astute and inquisitive shoppers (like you!) get the deal, not everyone. And the marketer gains something else—store traffic into the store or website—and in many cases—information about you or even a relationship with you.

And why do we respond to deals and discounts? The reasons are pretty simple and go back to the lessons of behavioral economics: We get more pleasure out of getting a good deal on something than simply paying a lower price. We see it as a win. We subconsciously equate price with value, so an item priced at $30 and discounted $10 is worth more than a $20 item. The $20 item is worth $20; the $30 item is worth $30, but we're getting a heck of a deal because it is $10 off.

You can see how the discount and deal approach is a win-win for everyone—the marketer gains a sale, more information, and an opportunity for more sales; you get a $30 beach towel, let's say, for $20.

Like Everything Else, the Internet Has Changed Everything

As described in the introduction, not too long ago, we had to depend on printed newspapers, periodicals, a good set of scissors, and an overstuffed drawer, purse, or pocket to get our "deals." Or we had to drive to the store to look for the "sale" signs in the window. There were other ways, but these were the primary channels for businesses to communicate their deals and discounts, and they were the primary channels for you to tune in.

It was a lot of work.

It has gotten a lot easier.

The Internet, of course, has changed the deal-seeking landscape forever. Real time ads and e-mails from businesses have become one heavily used medium, but even better, deal exchanges and portals have sprung up everywhere and have become the way to shop. There are hundreds—probably thousands—of them worldwide.

You can shop the morning newsletter. You can touch base daily (or weekly or even hourly!) with the portal site and search by product, by retailer, or by type of deal. You can simply cut to the chase by entering in what you're looking for, followed by the words "deal discount" (or "deal discount free") and your computer will take you right to the deal, either directly to its provider or to one of many portals where it appears—in an instant!

You may or may not find Internet-aided deal seeking to be productive—it can be time consuming, and you'll likely have to look at a lot of stuff you're *not* interested in. But like day trading or a reality TV show, it can be addictively fun!

And too, like a day trader, you'll have to decide on your style. Are you an addicted deal seeker looking every morning or sometimes several times a day to see what's out there? Or are you a "helicopter" shopper looking to drop in on certain deals for something specific you're looking for?

Either way, the Internet is a very compelling tool for the deal seeker. Most of what I present in this book comes from—or through—the Internet.

Leaving Digital Footprints

Freebie, deal, discount, and couponing sites do a lot more than just give you the better deal just to get you to buy something. We're talking about the digital world—and with every exchange of 20 percent off Pampers, there's also an exchange of data.

Most of these sites collect information on you when you sign up (and in most cases, you do) and collect more (free) information about your search and buying habits. This information is used not just to learn about you specifically but to learn about the shopping habits and profiles of large groups of people like you—all of which can be invaluable information to marketers.

The knowledge that you buy Pampers, of course, can go a long way toward determining other things you might be in the market for—but the marketer also learns your habits about price sensitivity, size preference, order frequency preference, and how you like to pay, beyond the fact that you buy diapers, period. This kind of information can be very hard to collect in a traditional multitier retail channel.

And don't worry; they're not just learning about you. They're also learning about people in your socioeconomic circle as a group. "Do young working parents in inner urban residences tend to buy the smaller size diaper package more often when the price is within *x* amount of the larger package?" might be a question answered by tracking digital footprints left by the active deal seeker.

So you get a valuable deal—or even free stuff. What they get could be priceless.

It's all part of the win-win.

Want a Special Deal? Be Part of a Group

The Internet gives us all a tremendous playing field for finding deals. But for the most part, it treats us like anonymous individuals all equal in their deal seeking. There may be some exceptions to this as browser cookies and "big data" marketing databases may identify us as interested golfers, cooks, readers, and so on based on our browsing habits—but for the most part, you and I will get the same results on a given deal search.

But there are ways to get to special deals, some familiar and some not so familiar, by joining groups. The most familiar are the American Automobile Association and the AARP. Marketers have long recognized the interests, loyalty, and economic power of these and other groups. Marketers are always looking to target a loyal clientele, who buy over and over again, and AAA provides a long list of relatively affluent travelers, while AARP gives access to millions of senior (and a few not-so-senior) citizens—a vibrant channel for offers of all sorts.

Other groups and associations you may want to be (or already be) a part of that draw deals and discounts include the following:

- *Professional or trade organizations.* Are you a doctor, lawyer, professional journalist, teacher, or part of some other profession? Or a union member? Drop the initials of AMA (American Medical Association), ABA (American Bar Association), ASJA (American Society of Journalists and Authors), or a related organization, and you may get a discount on insurance, travel, and much more.
- *Employers.* Certain large employers, especially in a given geographic area, will qualify you for a discount—employees of a large West Coast hospital chain get a 25 percent discount on AT&T Wireless services.

- *Military/government.* Most already employed here know this, but discounts for government employees, and especially military personnel and veterans, are abundant. What varies is whether they apply just to the employee or their family, just for active duty or retired personnel, or just for federal government employees or if they apply to state and local employees as well.

And of course, the largest and most obvious "group" hasn't even been mentioned—senior citizens! Senior discounts abound everywhere, as marketers see this key, growing, and often affluent group as a major opportunity. I'll talk more about senior and other major group discounts in Chapter 3 and will cover this special group in detail throughout the book.

Now You See It, Now You Don't: Evergreen vs. Temporal Offers

I'll come right out with it now. This is not an easy book to put together.

Why? With so many freebies, deals, and discounts out there, why would it be hard to put together such a book?

One reason is the sheer numbers. There are millions (well, I haven't counted) of offers at any given time.

But the bigger reason is this: most of the offers are what I call "temporal"—they're determined by time. "Free 6-inch sub when you buy one of equal value before June 1" is just such a temporal offer—it may only be good for a month. A week. A day. I've seen some offers good for only an hour.

So how do you capture these discounts in a book having a six-month publishing cycle?

The answer comes in two parts:

1. I will try to characterize the temporal discounts as best I can by example. Typically there is some consistency, as we see with periodic L. L. Bean 10 percent off coupons, Bed Bath & Beyond 20 percent off coupons, and so forth.
2. I will focus, wherever possible, on "evergreen" discounts—discounts, deals, and freebies that are pervasive through time—the best example being senior discounts.

So at best I will only give a flavor of the vast assortment of temporal discounts. But as I suggested in the introduction, I can't give you all the fish—but I can teach you *how to* fish for deals, discounts, and freebies as they come up.

It Never Hurts to Ask

I just turned 60.

Okay, happy birthday to me. So what's the point?

The point is that when I buy something, from a sports admission to an ice cream cone, people are starting to ask me how old I am. This actually started happening when I was about fifty-five, and at first, I thought it was kind of nosy. But the truth was far different—they were wondering if I qualified for their senior discount!

I caught on to this more slowly than some, but soon realized that I could turn this line of questioning around. Around to asking them: "Do I qualify for a senior discount?" "No, you have to be 62" or "you have to be 65" was often the answer, but "yes" was the answer often enough that I started to get into the habit.

The lesson is simple. If you're old—or *look* old—ask! No—it goes *way* beyond that. I'm sure it's happened to you—you went to buy something at the hardware store, and the cashier pulls out an ad circular giving 20 percent off on the very item you're buying—and you had no idea!

You should get into the habit of asking if any deals or discounts are available when you buy something. It's easy, and it's usually no skin off the salesperson's nose. Now don't take this too far—your dentist or ambulance driver will probably be put out or even annoyed by the question. Pick your battles. But there are a lot of winnable battles out there; after a while, it gets to be kind of fun (although somewhat against the typical American nonbarter culture, I know . . .)!

The Pitfalls of Deal Finding

Save 5, 10, 20 percent, or even get it for free. What a win! What more could you want?

To paraphrase Abraham Lincoln, deal finding works for some of the people some of the time, but not all the people all the time. Here are a few of the common pitfalls:

- *You'll buy stuff you don't need or want.* Maybe the eight-piece family dinner at Long John Silver's for $14.99 is a good deal (heck, a *two* piece dinner might run you half that), but you aren't looking for an eight-piece family dinner. Ditto for that great deal on that piece of furniture you don't need. I call it the "Costco Effect"—the tendency to load up with cartfuls of stuff you don't need just because it's cheap and it's there. A good idea is to decide if you need before you buy. A good test is to determine if there's any chance you'd buy it *without* the discount.
- *Saving money takes time.* You might grind up a whole lot of time looking for low-value free stuff, small discounts, or discounts that don't really fit—valuable time you could be spending walking your dog or helping your kids with

homework. Find a favorite deal site or two and stick with it—but not all day.

- *Obsessive deal finding might make you annoying.* I have a friend who, when we get together, must start off every conversation by telling me about the latest great hotel deal he got for his family. Interesting, but not so "top of mind" for me. Be aware that not all people want to hear about all the discounts all the time. You might get a reputation for being a cheapskate—or worse—for being boring!

The pitfalls are important but are merely a few dots to watch out for on an otherwise luscious deal-finding landscape. Keep your eyes open and your mind clear—and you'll almost certainly be rewarded with savings you never thought possible!

CHAPTER 2

Finding the Deal Online

Using Today's Tools to Search for Your Best Deals

It takes a lot of work to mine for gold—the real yellow metal, that is. But as you'll soon find after reading this chapter and this book, it isn't hard at all to find good deals on things—and even free stuff and services—on the Internet.

Gone are the days (well, not completely) where you'd have to scour newspapers, magazines, and ad circulars, scissors in hand, for all those coupons to cut out for stuff you might need, stuffing those little slips of paper in a drawer somewhere never to be seen again. You can still do this—if you're so inclined.

But the biggest problem with the clipping approach—other than its tendency to build calluses on the hands of its biggest users—was the fact that you had to take what was there—then *hope* you might need it or use it someday. Hence the calluses—and drawers, purses, and pockets stuffed with mostly outdated coupons—and you didn't really realize much saving *on stuff you needed* at the end of the day. Some of you might have easily been "couponed" into buying stuff you didn't need; others simply left the coupon unused, to be thrown away eventually.

Today's "process" on the Internet is better. You can browse coupon deals, usually presented daily on one of the portals described in the following sections or on many others (there are too many to describe them all). You can pick and choose what you want in a few minutes.

But better than that—if you're looking for children's clothing or a laptop computer or something else, you can easily hone in on deals and freebies *in that category*. Most of the better "deal" sites organize their offers by category, and some will send you e-mail newsletters aligned to certain categories of interest. Or you can cut to the chase by simply entering "deals discounts children's clothing" into your favorite search engine.

If only mining for that precious yellow metal was so easy.

The intent of this chapter is to give you some insight into how to "mine" for free stuff, and how to mine the best deals and discounts on the web. I teach you "how to fish" by giving some tips for the search, and I give some "fish" as examples, describing a few of the many sites available to help you in your quest.

I tend to like sites that are well organized and easy to use and that allow you to "filter" your way quickly into the stuff you want. If you do a search engine search for a product or service category, you will find many more sites available than what I've described. The bottom line? Pick and use the site that works best for you.

Freebies on the Web

It may surprise you, but there is an active and vibrant market for free stuff online. There are literally thousands of free sites and "free sample" pages out there, several of which function as portals to other ecommerce sites. Advertisers can post their wares, and in some cases, consumers can also post something they run across.

Most offer free samples, but some also alert consumers to test markets where they can receive free merchandise in exchange for a test or feedback, or they can receive some other compensation, like a gift card, for their participation.

Most of these freebies are low in value, and some may have no real dollar value at all—like a free brochure describing a product or service. But if you look through some of the larger freebie portals, you'll be surprised how much is really out there—and how easy it is to access.

To get the most out of the typical freebie portal, all you have to do is visit their web page. Most want you to sign up to "push" offers provided to them by their clients. Many of these offers appear on more than one freebie site, so you should only need to sign up for one or two to receive the best and most current offers.

Much of the "ad push" technology is simply based on giving your e-mail address to advertisers or groups of advertisers. Some of it is a bit more sophisticated—you might be told somewhere along the way to sign up for an ad engine like "Media Net" which will push "relevant advertising" your way based on cookies on your browser and by interest. These can work well—but can also overwhelm you—make sure you're really on board to receive offers before signing up for too much. This advice, of course, applies to deals and discounts as well as freebies.

Most sites recommend (and I do too)—creating a special "side" e-mail address for the purpose of receiving offers, as the amount of mail you might receive from individual advertisers might clutter or overwhelm a regular e-mail account. Typically you have some control over the kinds of offers you receive, and can, as a matter of routine maintenance, unsubscribe from what you don't want.

Here is a "free sample" of some of the freebie portals:

Hey, It's Free (heyitsfree.net)

Heyitsfree.net connects you to free offers of all sorts and is dedicated to the idea of making the search for freebies relatively routine, easy, and fun. After supplying a mailing address and an e-mail address (which they suggest not using your regular e-mail address due to possible overload with inbound offers), they make your contact info available to certain companies offering freebies. You receive "free" offers daily. Founder Ryan "Goob" Eubanks also specializes in identifying "birthday" freebies found within this site and further described in Chapter 3.

In Their Own Words

Hey, It's Free! (aka HIF) is a nationally recognized site dedicated to finding the best, legitimate freebies on the Internet while having a little fun along the way. I genuinely believe you'll find HIF to be one of the top sites to find 100% free consumer samples (aka freebies) and we have the awards to back it up!

Our number one goal is to filter out the spam, junk, and nonsense that clutter the freebie world and instead only post genuine freebies and samples. Our second goal is to have fun along the way by making goofy jokes about each freebie. Our third goal involves ordering nachos for lunch.

Hey, it's free!

They go on to say, *You won't get rich requesting freebies, but you'll get a lot of neat samples and you might start finding yourself getting excited to check the mailbox every day.*

Free Stuff Finder (www.freestufffinder.com)

Founded in 2006 by former go-go girl, motivational writer, and "obsessive-compulsive deal hunter" Tina (last name carefully not offered), Free Stuff Finder connects to a wide variety of freebies in sixteen categories plus a signup "VIP" option, which sets you up with a daily newsletter. There is plenty of material about searching for and finding free stuff as well. Beyond most freebie sites, which are typically United States only, Free Stuff Finder has extensions in Canada (www.freestufffinder.ca) and the United Kingdom (www.freestufffinder.co.uk).

In Their Own Words

Hey there! My name is Tina, also known as Free Stuff Finder. I'm an obsessive-compulsive deal hunter and couponer, and a mom of two little ones (aged 4 years and 10 months). Welcome to my world of savings!

And after a rather lengthy "Tina" bio, it goes on later on the page:

We share the latest freebies, samples, sales, and couponing deals every single day of the year. That's 365 days. Rain or shine, someone is always out finding the latest deals and posting them on the site. If there's a hot offer, you can be sure we'll report it here.

AllYou.com (www.allyou.com/budget-home/money-shopping/freebies)

The AllYou.com freebie page is a large and well-organized page within the larger deals and discounts portal AllYou.com. The page is organized into sections including Restaurants,

Desserts, Health and Beauty, Groceries, Family Fun, Travel, Classes, Workouts and Everything Else. Within each of these categories are several credible freebie offers, and in some cases, references to other money-saving ideas and information.

In Their Own Words

Simply put, *what's better than low cost? How about no cost! Here's how to score the most phenomenal freebies at grocery stores, the movies, restaurants and more.*

7 Retirement Mistakes Guide

Financial Engines

Whether you have saved $50,000 or $
guide written by the Financial Engines
Mistakes you can't afford to make".

Your Guide to the Best Freebies

What's better than low-cost? How about no cost! Here's how to score the most phenomenal freebies at grocery stores, the movies, restaurants and more.

MAIN | BIRTHDAY | RESTAURANTS | DESSERTS | BEAUTY | GROCERIES | MOVIES

TRAVEL | CLASSES | EXERCISE | EVERYWHERE

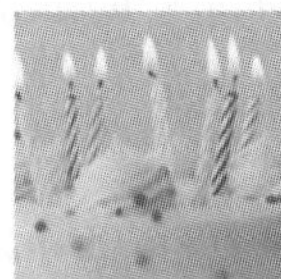

Freebie Guide: On Your Birthday
Get free stuff just for being born! These restaurants, retailers and more offer special discounts and freebies on your birthday.

Freebie Guide: Eat Free at These Restaurants
Join the membership programs at these 23 popular chains for a sign-up reward, no strings attached.

Freebie Guide: Desserts
Find out how to get the sweetest freebie of them all: free dessert!

Freebie Guide: Health and Beauty
Look even more marvelous with these free beauty products and health services.

Freebie Guide: Groceries
Cut down on your grocery bill by nabbing these exclusive freebies.

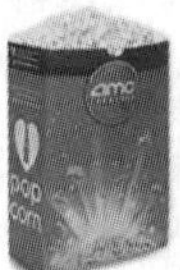

Freebie Guide: Family Fun
Going to the movies or your favorite museum doesn't have to come with an extravagant price tag.

Freaky Freddies (www.freakyfreddies.com)

FreakyFreddies.com lists samples in some 49 categories, from baby samples to vitamin supplements and almost everything in between. Catchy were the categories of "Romance Samples," "Teacher Stuff," and "Mystery Stuff," a hodgepodge of daily specials including a sample of One A Day TruNatal Vitamins from Walmart on the day I checked. The assortment of samples is broad and well organized on this site.

In Their Own Words

When a young man wanted to start a business more for a hobby in 1997, he had only a used computer, a small home office that was actually a bedroom, and the will to succeed.

When I first started there were only like twelve free stuff sites a round but now I guess about 5000. I give my success thanks to consumers and businesses supplying new freebies for everyone to enjoy. Today, FreakyFreddies.com the most popular free stuff sites on the Internet.

Samples.com

"Get Premium Samples" is the upfront slogan presented to site visitors as freebie portal Samples.com asks for your name and e-mail address to sign up "to receive offers and advertisements from our third party advertising partners." Samples can include anything from high-end health and beauty aids to nutritional supplements to a free 3M Microfiber Cleaning Cloth. This relatively simple and straightforward site does not have an "about us" page, so we don't know how they view themselves in their own words.

Dealing You In: Deal, Discount, and Coupon Portals

Not surprisingly, deal and discount portals offer online shopping deals sold directly and coupons and coupon codes to enable you to buy from the store you want. These sites function as marketplaces for merchandise and coupons and are typically tied into manufacturers and retailers, whose marketing organizations launch the deals. Most are temporal with expiration dates, or in the case of direct commerce, until the supply of product is gone.

Well-organized sites with a good search bar will get you to what you're looking for fairly quickly. Most dedicated "deal" sites, like Groupon and others, push coupons, coupon codes, and offers your way with daily updates and newsletters. Some actually link you directly to retailer sites or even eBay sellers offering good deals.

While most freebie portals are small mom-and-pop enterprises, deal, discount, and coupon portals run the range from small operators (mostly coupon portals) to large and even publicly traded enterprises like Groupon and RetailMeNot, some of which may actually handle some of the merchandise.

There may be some overlap between "freebie" portals and the ones listed below specializing in distributing discount coupons and deals, although I've found the discount portals to be larger and more sophisticated than the freebie sites. That's not a big surprise.

I should also note that "coupons" these days are generally not the old-fashioned little cut-out paper rectangles of yesteryear. Some are printable, usually with a barcode, but an increasing number these days are managed through a discount code used in a checkout process.

Groupon (www.groupon.com)

A publicly traded company, Groupon is one of the largest, if not the largest, coupon portals, self-described as highlighted below as building a "daily habit" in "local commerce" through a "vast mobile and online marketplace"—a place to "discover and save on amazing things to do, see, eat and buy."

Groupon allows you to browse hundreds—in some cases, thousands—of deals in "Things to Do," "Beauty & Spas," "Food & Drink," "Electronics," "Travel, Health & Fitness," and "Automotive"—a useful if perhaps broad categorization. Subcategories within these broader categories allow you to hone in more closely on the kind of deal you're looking for. The search bar is also a very effective navigation tool to cut to the chase.

The site is most likely the largest in terms of the number of deals offered, with nearly 8,000—10,000 deals at any given time. The deals tend to be for higher-quality items with larger discounts than many sites I looked at. The site is also an outlet for refurbished items, including a refurbished Apple MacBook Pro for some $500 off the list price at the time of this writing.

Bottom line Groupon is a complete shopping site for deals and discounts, not just a coupon or freebie site. Deal seekers should become familiar with this one. You may find yourself checking for Groupon deals before buying anything—many do. They do have a coupon page on the site as well in case you'd rather shop someplace else.

In Their Own Words

"Their own words" have a surprisingly "corporate BS" feel for such a consumer-friendly enterprise. Up front is the mission statement: *To connect local commerce, increasing consumer buying power while driving more business to local merchants through price and discovery.*

But then a description of "our company" gets us a little closer to what they do in plain English, still "corporate-y" but helpful: *Groupon is building the daily habit in local commerce, offering a vast mobile and online marketplace where people discover and save on amazing things to do, see, eat and buy. By enabling real-time commerce across local businesses, travel destinations, consumer products and live events, shoppers can find the best a city has to offer.*

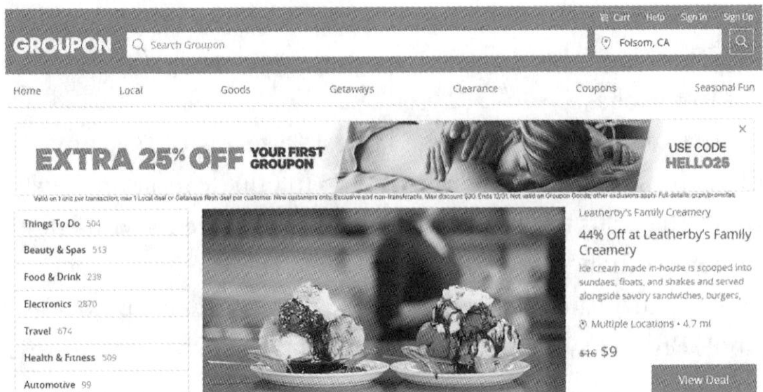

DealsPlus (www.dealsplus.com)

DealsPlus is a well-organized deal and discount portal offering deals in 27 categories, some general and some specific (like laptops). "Freebies" is one of the categories, so they play in this space too. Unlike other portals, many of the deals are offered by small resellers like those found on eBay.

The deals are organized by product or service category, and then there is another page of "Coupons" organized by retailer. A "Blog" page connects you with articles with consumer tips and deals and discounts, again in 13 categories of products and services.

I found DealsPlus to be particularly well organized and both broad enough and deep enough to be an efficient way to quickly find what you're looking for.

In Their Own Words

Tired of clipping coupons and scouring the internet for deals and promotional codes? So were we. And that's why on July 18th, 2006, we launched a website that makes it easy for shoppers to find and share the best deals and coupons. No hunting, no hassle, and no scissors required.

Welcome to DealsPlus, an online community of bargain hunters, tracking down the top deals and coupons and sharing them with each other online. To help out these dedicated deal finders, we've created a place where they can search, share, comment, and of course, save money. By simply signing in to DealsPlus, shoppers not only have access to thousands of deals and coupons posted by the community, but they are able to customize the way they browse, "plus" their favorite deals, follow their favorite members, and even subscribe to e-mail alerts for their favorite stores. Yup, it's that easy.

So, if you're looking to join more than 7 million monthly visitors who are saving tons of money by sharing deals and coupons from over 15,000 stores, then you're in luck. You've come to the right place.

Fun tidbits:

- *Each month, more than 7 million people visit DealsPlus*
- *Our members have shared 2,438,521 deals and 332,511 coupons*
- *210,708 people are following DealsPlus on Twitter*
- *540,442 people like DealsPlus on Facebook*

DealNews (www.dealnews.com)

DealNews is a general deal portal much like DealsPlus. In my opinion, it is not quite as broad or as well organized but has deals well worth the search. Major product/service categories include Clothing, Computers, Electronics, Home & Garden and a catchall "All Deals." A "Coupon" page connects you to coupon deals by chosen retailer. The orientation toward computers, electronics, and other such "hard goods" is notable, and the site is quite deep and wide within these categories—but pretty solid in clothing too.

Many of the "deals" are simply connections to existing discount retailers like Amazon and Adorama, some brought to the site by readers. Many of the listings show the comparative best price available elsewhere and describe how to get the best deals on shipping as you complete an order. There are also listings of refurbished products. A richly populated "Today's Hottest Deals" page and a newsletter round out the package.

In Their Own Words

Discovering the deals you want, at the moment you need them. Every day, DealNews brings you the best deals available on the Internet.

For consumers overwhelmed by the thousands of offers (and so-called offers) available online every day, DealNews provides a way to discover items that actually represent a great deal. DealNews' experts guarantee we'll only list products that are the lowest price available from reputable companies.

Our obsessive dedication to listing only the best deals is why DealNews.com is one of the top 1,000 most visited websites in the United States and read by tens of millions of deal-hungry consumers each month. Not bad for a site created way back in 1997, just so a couple of friends could share the great deals on cool gadgets that they were finding, right?

Statistics: 14.5 million visits per month, 19 years of deals, and over 400 deals every weekday.

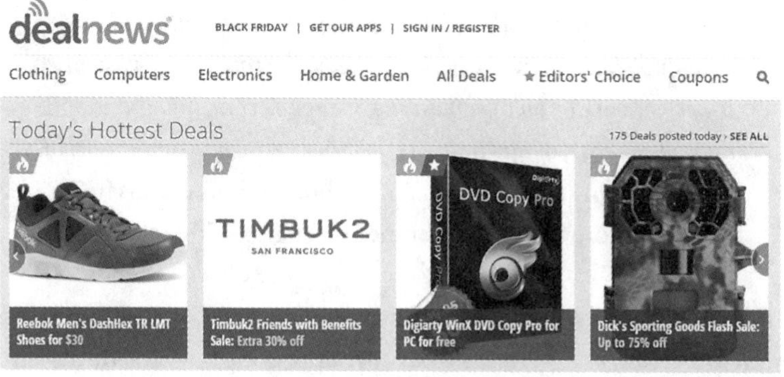

Coupons.com (www.coupons.com)

Coupons.com sets you up to search and print coupons or get coupon codes *by manufacturer or retailer* (as opposed to by product or service) for a vast assortment of stores and providers ranging from Krispy Kreme to Ralph Lauren and everything in between. You get coupons and deals for that retailer and suggestions for similar merchandise available at a discount from other retailers. If you like to shop or track deals at particular stores, such as Baskin Robbins or H&M or Nordstrom, this may be your site.

Most of the offers are temporal, tied to a certain product and "for a limited time only"—or until stock is gone. Discounts are substantial—typically 20 percent or more for the retailers I looked at (they have more than 100 on the site). There are some deals for discounted or free shipping as well.

The site encourages you to sign up for a weekly newsletter to learn about special deals and offers. A subsidiary site, "the-goodstuff," has offers for mostly higher-end food and household products. You can also link offers to certain debit and credit cards to get cash back or points from those cards.

In Their Own Words

We connect thousands of brands and retailers with millions of valuable consumers every day, whether through our vast publisher network or on our main site, Coupons.com, and our mobile apps. The reach of our industry-leading network is unparalleled.

Their own statistics claim $1.7 billion in transactions in 2015 covering more than 2000+ brands through 64,000 retail stores.

Savings.com (www.savings.com)

Savings.com is a general discount and coupon (discount) site offering over 200,000 coupons in 22 broadly defined categories. A good search tool allows you to search by product category or manufacturer—if you want an HP laptop, you'll get there quickly to find more than ten deals for this category/manufacturer combination.

Almost a legacy element in appearance, a separate "Grocery" page lets you "clip," or print, national electronic coupons on the products of your choice. They are subject to availability and usually in the $1- to $3-off range. The "Favado" subsidiary offers a mobile app that offers up "hand-selected" local electronic coupon savings from stores and other providers near you.

An account signup gets you a free weekly newsletter and a set of "editor's picks" deals.

In Their Own Words

Welcome to Savings.com! With over 200,000 current coupons and deals, we can help you spend less and live more.

RetailMeNot (www.retailmenot.com)

Not surprisingly, RetailMeNot serves mainly as a discount portal for retailers. Deals are presented daily by retailer, and those deals can include not only freebies but also free shipping and even gift card discounts—two categories not often singled out elsewhere. It's easy to find deals by retailer but you can also search by freebies, free shipping, gift card discounts, and across 24 categories of products and services. These product and service category pages are in turn organized first by retailer, then by specific coupons within that category.

The site also presents special holiday weekend sales on a separate page. The search bar allows quick access to deals on specific products and categories, and "joining" with an e-mail address and a zip code allows you to tap into local deals. Unlike most I've discussed before, RetailMeNot has extensive website and mobile operations in the international space, including Canada (retailmenot.ca) and the UK (vouchercodes.co.uk) as well as seven other European countries. RetailMeNot is a publicly traded company (ticker symbol "SALE").

In Their Own Words

Their "words" are more oriented to corporate clients than you, the consumer:

RetailMeNot is a marketplace that helps retailers and brands connect with millions of active shoppers anytime, anywhere to drive engagement and sales. With more than 600,000 coupons and offers for 70,000 retailers, we operate the world's largest marketplace for digital offers. We consistently innovate to offer new solutions that drive ROI for our retailers and brands, satisfy our consumers and create a top-rated workplace for our employees.

Statistics: 688 million visits in the last 12 months, 19 million unique mobile users, 45% of site traffic from mobile, and 49,000 email subscribers.

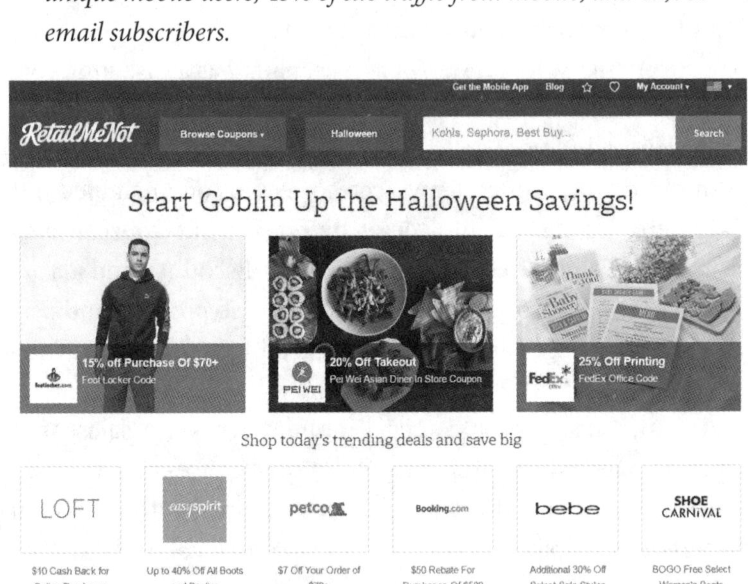

Krazy Coupon Lady (www.krazycouponlady.com)

Any site that can score me three string cheeses for free is worth a second look, and the whimsical if not-too-well-organized Krazy Coupon Lady site is a fun ride if nothing else. Why do I say "not too well organized?" The search tabs are located at the bottom of a ten-page long front page, and the "search" bar took me outside the site altogether for a search for laptops—a regular search on Google—instead of keeping me on the site (in fairness, that seems to be because they didn't have any deals on laptops that day).

The site seems to focus on the really good deals of the day, mostly for household products, from what's happening at Walmart to today's blowout deals on Pampers and Luvs diapers. I wouldn't recommend this one for targeted shopping for specific items or services, but a daily browse is interesting for those who have time for that sort of thing.

In Their Own Words

A national phenomenon . . . What started out as two eager young women shouting deals from their home computers has grown into a national phenomenon. Heather and Joanie have appeared on the Today Show, The Early Show, TLC, The Nate Berkus Show, Fox & Friends, and been featured in many national web and print articles. The two friends now run a highly successful company of women (and a few secure men), who work tirelessly to uncover the best deals in every category so that families everywhere can afford to live well! They continue to live by the mantra that "You'd be krazy not to be one of us!"

AllYou.com (www.allyou.com)

We return to AllYou, this time as a broader resource for deal seeking. This site, which appears to be a general deal/discount site that has moved more in the direction of freebies as described above, is most valuable as a general portal for savings advice and experiences. Listed are several articles and blogs sharing tips and experiences finding good deals. If you have a little extra time for some reading as you seek your deals and discounts, AllYou can help point you in the right direction.

Other Deal, Discount, and Coupon Portals

If you do a search engine search for "deals discounts coupons," you'll get an amazing 16,300,000 results. (Full disclosure: I didn't look at all of them!) Now of course that doesn't mean these are all "DDC" sites, but it gives you the idea (correctly) that there are a lot more sites out there and that this is a growing business.

I've listed some of the larger, broader, and better organized sites, but you may find others that suit your preference, or even your niche (such as www.allnaturalsavings.com) for deals on natural foods. A look at SmartSource, LivingSocial (which specializes in local deals), FreeShipping.org (which specializes, not surprisingly, in free or reduced shipping deals), Offers.com, Deal Locker, Fat Wallet (an online community of experienced deal seekers), and many others can get you suitably immersed in the productive pastime of deal hunting.

Happy shopping!

CHAPTER 3

Getting in with the Group

Senior and Other Group Deals

At the risk of repeating myself, I just turned 60.

That makes me (sort of) part of a group. Sort of? Well, especially in today's era, where "60 is the new 40," I don't really feel like a "senior citizen"—and in most circles, indeed I'm not. Most—including the federal government—define "seniors" as 65 and over.

Okay, so do I have to wait another five years to qualify for a senior discount? In most circles, yes. But marketers love groups, and they love groups with money to spend. And as a late-blooming boomer, I just might fall into *that* category of well-to-do spenders, no?

They hope I do, anyway. So there's a constant and persistent effort to reel me in through deals and discounts. And that's a good thing.

Marketers and Sellers *Love* Groups—Why?

Because they're there? Heck no. Marketers and sellers love groups like seniors, almost-seniors, AAA members, professional teachers, and so on because they, first of all, have disposable income (well I know some teachers who would argue that). But the bigger reason, for the most part, is that they can *target* the group with promotions, offers, and the more general concept of their brand.

Marketers love targeted groups because of efficiency. They can design a message for that group—and likely generate more interest (a higher "hit rate") from that group. Ever notice the preponderance of drug commercials on evening news programs? It's because more older people get their news by watching TV, and older people typically have more health problems requiring fancy pharmaceuticals.

I'm not out to emphasize the infirmities of the elderly—but rather to say that businesses and organizations that want to sell more product have gotten real smart about targeting such groups with deals and discounts.

Get the business—and the loyalty—of a well-off "senior" couple, and they will fly your airline or stay in your hotel chain or eat in your restaurant forever—so goes the logic. And they may go further to recommend your "property" to other seniors, as well as their families and other "younger" folks. After all, seniors are still respected these days (I hope!) for their wisdom!

A Golden Age—Senior Discounts Are Everywhere

That all said, many businesses simply look at senior discounts as the "right thing to do"—a gesture of respect and thanks for older folks that have "made it" to their golden years. We applaud this notion too, but that said, being a senior brings a lot of the right kind of attention from marketers.

Do a search on "senior discount," and you'll get about a million and a half hits. And many of these "hits" are lists of senior discounts others have already researched and reported on! Bottom line, there are lots of opportunities out there—opportunities to save and, for many, make your retirement dollars stretch further.

Oh, and one more thing: you should never assume you're too young to be a "senior"! Although the "classic" definition of senior is age 65 and up, many well-established discounts are offered to people as "young" as 50. AARP memberships are for those 50 and older.

And if the discount isn't so well-established, for instance, if it's a teen ticket taker at the local high school football game—you may well qualify simply for having enough gray hair. If the discount isn't etched in stone, folks interacting with a customer like to "do them good." It's worked often for me. Don't be ashamed to ask—and you may not even have to.

How to Research Senior Discounts

The best ways to research senior discounts are as follows:

1. *Search online.* This works best for national discounts from national chains, everything from airlines to restaurants to hotels to retailers to health services providers. As I'll describe below, you can go directly to a seller's website or to a senior discount portal, or you can subscribe to a newsletter. I'll describe online deal seeking in the following.
2. *Ask.* Especially for local businesses and organizations—and for "unlisted" deals—not only does it not *hurt* to ask but in my experience, most often you'll succeed! *Assume* that they have a deal for you—most do. You might be surprised to find that that plumber who just soaked you for $250 for

that drain cleaning is only too happy to offer a 10 percent senior discount on the service if you ask.

3. *Become part of a senior "group."* To be a senior, normally all you have to do is be of a certain age—and your ID will do if you need anything at all. But as I'll describe, it helps to be part of a group—you may get better discounts, and it'll be easier to find them. Join AARP (which I'll describe below) or SeniorCircle, or sign up for a premium membership at seniordiscounts.com, and you're likely to find out about better deals and discounts.

Caveat Senior: Pitfalls and Other Stuff to Be Aware Of

There aren't many caveats to senior discounts. Most are upfront, transparent, and—as mentioned earlier—evergreen. They're often not the deepest discount, but they're always there and can always be counted on—no time limits, no expiration dates, no "BOGO" or other ties to buying something.

But there are a few downsides to be aware of:

- *Senior discounts may not always be the best deal.* Generally speaking, senior discounts are 10 to 15 percent—not bad but in many states it does little more than save the sales tax (not a bad thing, mind you!). But most are written so as not to be combinable with other discounts and deals. So if your favorite Hilton is offering 20 percent for a weekend stay but only a 10 percent senior discount, which one should you take? Got it. The message is, don't quit looking for other deals and discounts just because someone offers a senior discount.
- *Senior discounts may not be available consistently across a chain.* Many businesses, which appear to be national chains with consistent policies everywhere, are in fact not—they

are federations of franchisees. And not every franchisee is contractually committed to offering the "deal." You'll find this a lot in the hotel and rental car space: "We don't offer that discount." Of course, they may offer something better too. Particularly if the national website says something like "discount varies," make sure you ask about the discount before assuming it will happen.

- *Other caveats apply*. The caveats about deal making generally apply to senior discounts. Don't go for something you don't need—or can't afford—just because of the discount. A short term "win" can become a longer term loss in a hurry.

Senior Discounts Online

Most senior discounts are evergreen and thus don't require much searching (you can always get 10 percent off at Best Westerns if 55 or older, so once you figure this out, there's nothing to research). But you'll need to find them in the first place, especially for purchases outside your normal routine. As usual, there are websites for this; the Internet makes it easy. There are three simple ways to research senior discounts online:

1. Search "senior discount" by item or service (and locale if appropriate)—"senior discount car wash Denver CO" will likely find what you seek.
2. Search the business or organization website for a senior discount page or listing. Examples might be "Southwest Airlines senior discount deals" or "Wendy's senior discount deals." I've found most national chain businesses with a senior discount will have a page on their site devoted specifically to the senior discount; sometimes it appears as an item on a larger listing of available discounts.

3. Use a senior discount portal. Like Groupon and DealsPlus and other portals described in Chapter 2, there are portals specializing in senior discounts and deals; three of them are described below with a fourth "app" for the technologically intrepid.

Free4Seniors.com

"Helping Citizens over 50+ Save Money" is the slogan of this relatively simple site. The original focus was freebies, which on the day I checked it out, offered free popcorn at an AMC theater and a free sample of Monistat Chafing Relief among about a dozen offers on the main freebie page. But other pages link to "Free Walmart Coupons," "Free Grocery Coupons," "Free Baby Coupons" (for seniors, really?) and "Free Samples by Mail"—giving a fairly rich assortment of free stuff to choose from.

There is also a more traditional "senior discounts" page listing many of the typical discounts available for travel, restaurants, and other needs and wants. There's a pretty good set of summary listings for AARP discounts on everything from hotels to hearing aids.

The site navigation and layout is so-so at best (e.g., it opens new pages when you want to see a list, a senior user may try unsuccessfully to use the back button and may end up with ten windows open at the end of a session), but with my standard browser settings, the type size was larger than normal, probably an advantage for some seniors.

In Their Own Words

Welcome to Free4Seniors—the original tool to help those age 50+ save money. Find the latest coupons, discounts, deals and freebies to help you live better in the best years of your life.

seniordiscounts (www.seniordiscounts.com)

"It's what you deserve" is the apt slogan of this site, which claims to offer the "largest directory of senior discounts with 'over 250,000 local listings.'"

The drop-down menu (which again might be hard for seniors to find) lists more than 25 categories of products and services and allows you to input a location. The listings very clearly spell out the discount, the age requirement, and the geography where it applies (usually "nationwide"). I searched "Computers and Internet" in my zip code and got a lot of offers for computer services and training—my favorite was "Char Wood the Computer Granny"—a Florida service offering free beginner to intermediate computer lessons by e-mail to those over 50 nationwide.

The navigation may take some getting used to but the presentation is excellent. Weekly newsletters and three levels of membership round out the offerings. Users can submit offers they find. One appealing feature: you can change the font size easily by clicking the "Text Size: A+ A-" buttons right at the top of the page.

In my opinion, this is the best dedicated senior discount and deal site.

In Their Own Words

It's a bit dry and targeted to advertising businesses:

SeniorDiscounts.com is an online directory of US businesses that offer discounts to people 50 years of age and older. We currently list over 150,000 business locations, which include the contact information, discount information and other information necessary to receive each discount.

We strive to provide the most complete and accurate listing of all age-related discounts for goods and services.

The Senior List (www.theseniorlist.com)

The Senior List is a portal and help site with several categories of help for seniors, from help with Alzheimer's and other health issues to in-home care to legal advice. The section we're interested here is the Discounts page—which instead of including information organized by topic into pages, includes articles listing senior discounts. The Best Senior Discounts of 2016 section contains articles and lists on groceries, restaurants, cell phones, and mobile medical alert systems, to name a few.

While I found the navigation a bit cumbersome—especially for a senior apprehensive about computers and the Internet, the content is helpful and insightful. Even more helpful is the apparent editorial review and verification of the discounts; "verified" in red letters appears next to each discount if the editors found it to be accurate. That Fred Meyer offers a 10 percent discount the first Tuesday of every month is a useful tidbit—although that one was pretty easy to find on their website too—and their website lists exclusions and exceptions that may apply.

Sciddy

Sciddy apparently started out as a website, but is now set up exclusively as an Apple or Android app. It's designed to not only serve as a portal to senior discounts on food, entertainment, travel, home services, and other categories but also use location mapping to notify you of available senior discounts when you're in an establishment. Not all seniors are inclined to use apps, but this one is easy to use, and it's free.

The Organization Man—and Woman

It's no secret—groups of people have more buying power than individual people. And as mentioned earlier in the book, marketers and sellers are dying to target their wares toward groups of interest who are more likely to take them up for their offers.

As a result, literally millions of deals lie in wait for AARP and AAA members, government and military employees, union members, teachers (and their students), lawyers and other professions, college alumni, and almost any other group you can think of.

The point is—if you're part of anything, and most likely you are—it doesn't hurt to try. The Internet makes it easy, and it's also easy to ask at the point of sale. The worst thing that can happen is the two-word answer: "No, sorry." It won't ruin your day.

Starting at the Beginning—AARP

The biggest organizational conduit I've found for deals and discounts—and a few freebies—is the venerable AARP. For $16 annually, you can join and open your door to numerous discounts plus a lot of other features, services, news, and wisdom worthwhile to most seniors. In theory, you have to be 50 to be eligible for membership—but they once sent my son a membership invitation when he was 8 years old!

The 50-year age requirement is a good thing though—you can realize a wide variety of senior benefits and discounts at age 50 simply by coughing up $16 a year (spouses younger than 50 qualify too). For most of us, that pays off after one dinner for two at the Outback Steakhouse (15 percent discount!).

The main page is at www.aarp.org, of course, and you can cut to the chase and view the available discounts at www.aarp.org/benefits-discounts/services_discounts_list/.

Most discounts range from 5 to 20 percent, with some insurance and other programs tailored to special needs and special programs like free tax preparation. Most discounts are offered in affiliation with AARP; you leave the main AARP site to see the details on the AARP Member Advantages website, which presents each offer in a standard format. It can take a while to shop through these discounts.

- *Travel benefits.* Includes a large assortment of tours, cruises, and car rental offerings.
- *More travel benefits.* Discounts at some 49 hotels and hotel chains (although some are of the same family, such as Hilton). See Chapter 11 for more on hotel discounts.
- *Apparel, auto, and home.* Includes the AARP Auto Buying Program and several auto service offerings, as well as special rates for a couple of home security monitoring services.
- *Dining and entertainment.* There are fifteen restaurants listed here and also Ticketmaster and Regal Cinemas and Cirque de Soleil. Good deals include 15 percent off every day at Outback Steakhouse, 10 percent at Chart House, and 25 percent at Ticketmaster on purchases of 4 tickets.
- *Electronics.* Cricket Wireless, AT&T, Kindle e-books, and ancestry.com are on this list.
- *Flowers and gifts.* Deals and discounts for flowers, cookies, chocolates, and gift cards.
- *Groceries and coupons.* A small assortment of specialty food and home delivery providers.
- *Health and wellness.* An assortment of health, fitness, prescription, vision care, dental, and even pet insurance offerings.
- *Health discounts and insurance.* Medicare supplement plans.
- *Vehicle, life, and property insurance.* Includes Hartford Auto Insurance Program with special senior-tailored features, homeowners insurance, boat insurance, and even motorcycle insurance.

- *Programs.* A catchall category that includes such freebies as the AARP Foundation Tax-Aide, where you can get taxes filed for free if income is less than $62,500 and other qualifications are met.

If you're 50 and over, AARP is an excellent conduit for discounts and deals—well worth the $16 membership. It's worth noting that AARP operates in Canada, Mexico, and other countries with slightly higher annual fees but similar benefits.

Traveling the World with AAA

"The Sale is Always On" crows the discounts page of the American Automobile Association, or "AAA." Indeed, through their discounts and rewards program, they claim "savings today" with "over 100,000 retail, service and travel discounts."

The most common of these discounts, honored almost everywhere you go, is the 10 percent discount on lodging. If the hotel is AAA rated, the discount is a no-brainer. But I've flashed my AAA card at check-in counters with no AAA affiliation whatsoever and been given the discount—probably because they know you'll "walk" and stay at the next hotel down the street.

The easy-to-navigate discounts page that can be accessed via www.aaa.com/discountsandrewards gets you to discounts and offers in eight categories: Automotive (no surprise!), Entertainment and Attractions, Home & Business, Personal Services, Restaurants, Shopping, Travel, and International.

Dropdown menus then give five to ten more subcategories. Dropping down from Personal Services, for instance, gave categories including Barbershops & Hair Salons, Day Spas, Dry Cleaning, Eye Care, Fitness Centers, Hearing Aids, Medical Equipment, Pharmacies, and Translators. A tour through Dry Cleaning, however, came up dry (no discounts available), but the

AAA Prescription Savings Program can save up to 75 percent on prescriptions not covered by insurance.

Not surprisingly, most of the discounts tended to be in the Automotive, Travel and Entertainment sections.

What I like best about AAA discounts is that they are typically evergreen—that is, always available. And unlike AARP, there is no age distinction—you're eligible whether you're 16 or 60. There is a tab on the main discounts page for "Limited Time Offers" with deals on everything from a Dell computer to 30 percent off on the Moscow Ballet's *Great Russian Nutcracker*.

The AAA membership costs $56 a year (single membership) but you get a lot for that—roadside service, maps, DMV services, travel services. Most sellers require a AAA card and/or membership number.

We Want You—Military, Veterans, and Government Discounts

Most military and government workers have already discovered the fact that they're eligible for a wide assortment of discounts. These folks comprise a very large buying group, and particularly in the case of active and retired military, a lot of organizations look at a discount as a token of appreciation (and good public relations as well.)

Military and government discounts are particularly abundant for travel and services such as cell phones but cover the range of fitness centers, electronics, household goods, automotive, and so forth.

Most active duty military and actively employed federal employees are eligible for these discounts. What varies by seller is the availability of discounts and deals for spouses, retired, and immediate family members—these eligibilities can expand the value of the discount *a lot*—it's worth checking before you buy. Also, the eligibility for state and local government employees varies.

Like many other discounts, it pays to research, if by no other means, by searching "laptop computer military discount" or "hotels New York City government discount" or some such—you'll identify these discounts fairly quickly. Or you can use the portals mentioned in the following sections.

And don't forget that it never hurts to ask. Even if a seller doesn't have a government or especially a military discount on the books for you—they may make one up on the spot.

Portals and Websites

MyMilitarySavings.com is a deal, discount, and coupon portal targeted to active and retired military and their families. A free membership gains access to thousands of coupons and deals, most for smaller items you can buy at military commissaries. In fact, most of the deals are through the commissaries, which already have some pretty good deals without the coupons.

In their own words,

> *For over 25 years, we have worked creatively to bring specialized savings and consumer promotions directly to the active and retired Military families worldwide via an array of in-store coupons and displays.*

GovX (www.govx.com) is a portal offering exclusive discounts on more than 60,000+ products mainly targeted at retired military and government workers. A free membership gives access to the site, which is closed to those without memberships, so I was unable to examine the specifics.

In their own words,

> *GovX is for ALL Who Have Served: Current and Former Military, Law Enforcement, First Responders and Related Government*

Employees. Let us support your life after work with exclusive discounts. Never pay retail again.

Militarybenefits.info is a general information portal targeted to military, retired military, and veterans. Their "discounts" page leads to a wide assortment of well-organized offers, deals, and discounts.

I'm a Member—Trade and Professional Groups and Associations

Are you a teacher? A student? A physician? An airline pilot? An Ohio State graduate?

The list goes on. You *must* be somebody, right?

And if you are part of one of these professional groups or the trade, professional, alumni, or some other association behind them—or an employee of a big company—you're likely to be eligible for deals and discounts.

For example, the blog at giftcardgranny.com lists 82 ("The Complete List") of teacher discounts. Many of them are on things related to the process of educating—like books or free PBS videos. But there are plenty of discounts not only for craft stores (15 percent off at Michaels or Joann's, for instance) and office supply and other stores but also for museums such as the Art Institute of Chicago, entertainment destinations such as Legoland, or even car insurance—and many others. What's interesting about the teacher discounts is that they are bigger (typically 15 percent) and for quality bigger-ticket items—no offers for a buck off on your next purchase of macaroni and cheese, thank you.

The lesson is clear—even if you aren't a teacher. Figure out who you are and search for the discounts provided for others like you—and you're likely to find something.

You'll never be told to sit in the corner for trying.

It's Your Birthday? You're Part of a Group

It's happened to all of us. We go out for our birthday to enjoy a nice dinner. Dinner over, yummy, that was good—and now it's time to leave.

Suddenly, loudly, and out of nowhere appear all the floor staff of the restaurant (and then some), dancing and strutting your way with a beautiful little cake with a lit candle in the center. And they chant—and start to sing loudly—*Happy birthday to you, happy birthday to you*—in whatever language is germane to the restaurant you're in.

You just got a birthday freebie.

Turns out, that's not hard to do. And for that special day, some of them are worth a lot more too, like 20 percent off at Columbia Sportswear or Land's End online or a free ticket to see the Baltimore Orioles.

Of course, there are a few lists out there. My favorite is put together by the Hey, It's Free guy—Ryan "Goob" Eubanks—whom we met in the last chapter.

His birthday freebies page (www.heyitsfree.net/birthday-freebies/) has hundreds of freebies—most but not all from restaurants. Most are free desserts, but sometimes you get the whole meal, such as at Denny's or Perkins, or at Benihana, you get a free $30 gift certificate with the purchase of a second entrée.

So if you're about to "turn the page" into another year, check out these freebies first!

You'll have something else to celebrate.

The Wide World of Deals—You'll Never Use them All

Summing up—there are literally thousands of freebies and discounts out there. And I haven't even covered loyalty programs, corporate discounts, advance purchase discounts, or quantity discounts, to name a few. But once you get in the habit of thinking "freebie," "deal," or "discount"—and once you become familiar with the tools and tactics to find them—naturally, you'll get good at it, and you'll find deals that I've never heard of or thought of.

To put it in corporate-speak, it's a mindset or a thought process you'll adopt quickly if you don't have it already. You'll learn to search. You'll learn to ask. You'll learn that this is a game, a creative game, with no rules or boundaries.

Parts II and III of this book are next and describe some (a sampler, really) of the thousands of freebies, deals, and discounts I've become familiar with.

Live long, have fun, and happy deal hunting.

Part II

Necessities and Needs

Freebies, Deals, and Discounts
for the "Musts" in Life

CHAPTER 4

Staying Healthy for Less

Freebies and Discounts on Health and Health Care Services

In this day and age, with skyrocketing health care costs, one doesn't naturally think long and hard about how to get such services for free—or for less than the going rate. Part of the reason—for personal health care anyway—is that many of us are covered by insurance and don't have to. But many of us are not; additionally most insurance coverages leave expenses on the table for us to pick up anyhow.

Further, there are categories of health expenses not covered by traditional health plans—over-the-counter medicines to begin with and moving laterally as well into eye care, dental care, and even veterinary services (yes, that counts as health too—just for our four-legged friends!)

This chapter will help you become a better shopper for health services of all sorts, including clinical medical services, prescription and over-the-counter drugs, vaccinations, and immunizations—and for dental, vision, and veterinary care too.

Medical Services

Free Stuff and Services

"Free" health care has actually been the subject of extensive debate for years; in particular, whether there should be a government single payer for all health needs as is found in many other countries. I won't take up that debate here.

But I will point out that free health services and drugs are often available if you keep your eyes open. Some of these services are offered only to lower income levels. But many are offered to the general public.

- *Free and sliding-scale clinics.* If you're looking for basic clinical services such as basic medical or dental screening, vaccinations, mammography, and other services, a good way to find them is to search for "free health services (your city)" or use a portal like FreeClinics.com. The portal FreeClinics.com (www.freeclinics.com) points you to such free clinics in your area. Some clinics are completely free; some operate on a "sliding scale," where the fees may depend on a patient's income. In their own words, *We have done our best to scour the Internet, nonprofit organizations, yellow pages, medical websites, to find the most complete list of free medical clinics on the Internet.*
- *Free services through churches and community centers.* Local community centers and churches may offer free clinics occasionally to give shots and do medical screenings, diagnostics, dental screenings, mammographies, and other health services for free. The Touched Twice Lake County's free health care clinic hosted by the Oakwood

Community Church in Waukesha, Wisconsin, is but one example. Again, you can find these by searching for "free health services" in your area.

- *HRSA—Health Resources and Services Administration.* Tens of millions get affordable health care and other help through this arm of the U.S. Department of Health and Human Services mainly for those unable to pay. At HRSA health centers, you "pay what you can afford" for checkups and treatments. See findahealthcenter.hrsa .gov/index.html.

  One service, the so-called "Hill-Burton" law, passed in 1946, gave financial help to hospitals and health care organizations to build facilities in exchange for free or reduced cost services for those unable to pay. About 150 health care facilities nationwide are still obliged to provide these services. Families of four with an income under $24,300 are eligible. See www.hrsa.gov.

- *Patient assistance programs.* Patient assistance programs are run by pharmaceutical companies to provide free medications to those who can't afford to buy and who don't have prescription drug coverage elsewhere. Most are offered as a public relations exercise on the part of the pharma company.

  The portal RxAssist (www.rxassist.org) provides a resource and comprehensive database to search for specific drugs and drug programs offered by pharma companies. The site provides information, then typically routes you directly to the pharma company's assistance website, such as Pfizer's "RxPathways" or equivalent or to another collective assistance portal.

  For example, the recently controversial EpiPen, epinephrine emergency anaphylaxis treatment offered by

Mylan, can be obtained for free (as the company recently claimed before Congress) for qualifying patients at or below 400 percent of the federal poverty line. "Free," however, does not account for the substantial paperwork you may have to do to qualify for and receive these products!

- *Drug trials*. Particularly if you already have a specific malady such as arthritis or diabetes, you can set yourself up to receive free medications for one of the thousands of clinical drug trials big pharma companies have to run every year.

  Some trials simply involve dispensing medications over a period of time; others involve diagnostics or evaluation of complementary treatments. The drugs and treatments are generally safe, as they have already been tested extensively in the laboratory. Phase 1 and Phase 2 trials have some risk, but the risk is mitigated by the extensive lab trials, the reputation of the pharma company, and insurance. Phase 3 trials are virtually risk free. Furthermore, the treatment is halted if any risks become apparent. You are made fully aware of the anticipated benefits—and risks and possible side effects—of the drug. You get the added benefits of receiving new and potentially better treatments before others, the general satisfaction of knowing you're helping the population having your maladies, and in some cases, compensation.

  Portals are available to connect you to clinical drug trials. Clinical Connection (www.clinicalconnection.com) allows you to search by keyword and zip code through more than 120,000 active clinical trial listings. A recent search for "gout" trials returned eleven studies, one of which is being conducted in 59 locations across the country. A search under Parkinson's disease returned 131 studies and trials.

You can also do a search yourself—for example, "arthritis drug trials."

- *Over-the-counter medications.* As you likely know, prescription drugs are not the only expensive items on the druggists' shelves. The cost of over-the-counter meds like cough syrup, anti-inflammatories, stomach meds, skin care products, and so forth can also add up. Free samples can be easily found at freesamples.org and other freebie portals. Local assistance events like the recent NCMedAssist (www.medassist.org) can also be a resource to the lower income qualified.

Senior Discounts

Most of the freebies and discounts noted in this section are available and widely used by seniors. In addition, AARP is a major source of discounts for health products and services, and some of the health insurers and pharmacies have recognized this important market.

- *AARP* offers a series of supplements and enhancements to Medicare through the large insurer United Healthcare. Medicare Advantage combines Parts A (hospital coverage) and Part B (doctor coverage) into a single plan often with drug benefits woven in. The AARP version may have modest cost advantages but offers enhanced benefits too—many for a zero copay and additional benefits, such as annual hearing exams and hearing aid benefits. Through their "Benefits and Discounts" page, AARP also acts as a portal to a number of health products and services, ranging from 30 percent off of eyewear at LensCrafters to up to 61 percent off on prescription drugs through OptumRx.

Other Deals and Discounts

The demand for health products and services generally exceeds the supply, so in a large measure, marketers don't have to price aggressively to make their sales goals. That said, there are ways to effectively bypass full-price products and services, often by siding with those with buying power, such as the big insurance companies; by finding out ways to cut middlemen; or by even leaving the country, where, as everybody knows and for whatever reason, health care is generally less expensive.

- *Discount prescription portals.* Several pharmacy benefits providers operate portals to provide prescriptions and vaccinations/immunizations at deep discounts or sometimes even free. Discounts can be up to 75 percent, and in some cases, if income qualified, prescriptions can be free. They are often supplied by pharma manufacturers selling in bulk or giving away free drugs as a public relations exercise.

  As an example, the "discount prescription purveyor" portal HelpRx (www.helprx.com) offers 50,000 medications at up to 75 percent off "list" price to registered members. Some portals require a modest membership fee, maybe $35 per month, but purvey their drugs to income-qualified members for free (e.g., see SCBN Prescription Advocacy at www.scbn.org). Some, such as HelpRx, have no fees, and the discounts can be used at your local pharmacy as well.
- *Over-the-counter drug discounts.* You can drop into one of the discounts and deals portals, such as DealsPlus or DealNews, and search for a specific product or under "health and beauty" and see a lot of deals—though the health and beauty search was quite biased toward

the "beauty" side. Coupons.com offered coupon deals on a number of OTC products such as Bayer aspirin, but the savings were minor—a buck here, a buck and a half there.

- *Medical tourism.* Need a hip or a knee replacement? Back surgery? Cosmetic surgery or LASIK (which is typically not covered by insurance)? Willing to travel? Don't have insurance, or have insurance but a ridiculously high deductible or copay? You might be a good candidate for doing it overseas. Mexico, Thailand, Turkey, India, Dubai, Peru, and Central America are all low cost and mostly pleasant places to visit, and you can get a knee replacement, which might cost $50,000 here done for $15,000 or so overseas. The providers are highly professional for the most part—they know they're being judged against a high standard. A search for "medical tourism" will bring you to several portals, many of whom act as travel agents as well. MedRetreat (www.medretreat.com) is a good example.

Dental Care Deals and Discounts

Those of us long familiar with what seem like endless dental procedures and bills will relish the fact that some relief exists. You don't have to simply buy dental insurance on the open market (bravo if you get it from your employer)—which, with its limitations, copays, and caps, seems to cost almost as much as the benefit you receive. So-called "dental savings plans," where you buy into a discount platform often matching the rates dentists bill insurance can cut costs dramatically especially for major procedures. If you're willing to travel a bit and have your work done by someone other than a U.S. licensed dentist, you can save up to 50 percent by going to a dental school or going overseas.

- *Dental discounts.* Ordinarily I'm not a big fan of discount "clubs" that require you to pay an annual fee to receive what may be uncertain discounts for stuff and services you may not really need. But the inevitability and cost of dental work makes some of these plans attractive. Health insurer Aetna offers a "Vital Savings" dental savings plan for as little as $141 per year; the savings range from 10 to 60 percent, with such services as a routine checkup costing $37 instead of $91 (on average); a root canal costing $392 instead of $1,061; or an implant costing $1,482 instead of $2,300. The savings are attributable to the buying power of Aetna and likely match the contract rates they use for their insurance programs; 161,000 dentists nationwide participate. Interestingly, the price is the same regardless of age; additionally there are no waiting periods or limitations for preexisting conditions (www.aetnadentaloffers.com or 855-336-7742).
- *Dental schools.* If you happen to be located near a major university that has a dental school, you can often get routine and not-so-routine dental care at reduced cost or even free. The Ohio State University College of Dentistry offers everything from basic teeth whitening to root canals to implants and emergency care at their on-campus dental clinic and advanced dental clinics at what they estimate to be half of the normal cost. They warn that appointments take longer, and of course, students will be doing the work—but under the supervision of faculty dentists. For similar services in your area, just search "dental clinics" and the school name. Community or specialty colleges offering dental hygiene programs may also offer discounted or even free services.

- *Dental tourism.* Need a couple of implants and a root canal? Might as well make a vacation out of it! You can save 40 to 60 percent on the dental work—which more than pays for the vacation. If you go to the Dent-Art Center in Tijuana, Mexico, the dentist's mother will pick you up at the San Diego airport to take you across the border. The service and treatment are excellent, and they'll drive you three blocks (or you can walk) to the four-star Hotel Lucerna for $88/night to lay by the pool to rest up from your procedure. As they have a 24-hour dental lab right on the premises, you can get a crown in an overnight stay—no temporary crowns, no two-week wait. And you'll save as much as 60 percent and be treated like you own the place (www.dent-artcenter.com). A search for "dental tourism" or a look through the Patients beyond Borders portal will help you find a provider. Some portals act more as travel agents, setting up your travel and lodging almost as if your dental (or medical) procedure was a vacation.

Vision Care

In a large measure, eye care is a little different than the other health professions in that the end product is an object used to correct vision—glasses or contacts usually. These products, unlike those in the medical and dental space, can be produced easily and rather cheaply—so there is a lot of competition. That competition leads to a number of freebies and discounts.

Free Stuff and Services

The most common freebie in the eye care space is the eye exam, which is often tied to the purchase of glasses or contacts. The "eye-dea" of course is to get you in the door.

- *Free eye exam.* For most suppliers of corrective eyewear, the eye exam is like the "check engine light" in an auto repair shop—except most major U.S. eyewear suppliers give one for free (normally $50 to $75). Now it's typically only a refractive exam—it tests for correction but not overall eye health. And most require the subsequent purchase of eyeglasses if indicated by the exam. Still, this can save you money, especially if you haven't had an eye exam recently.

  For seniors, a special program called the "Seniors EyeCare Program" exists and is sponsored by the Foundation of the American Academy of Ophthalmology. Volunteer ophthalmologists give free eye exams to seniors (over 65) with no insurance and no previous visits in the last three years. (See www eyedoctorguide.com/eye_care/free_senior_eye_exams.html.)

Senior Discounts

The best senior discounts appear to be through AARP—as in the 30 percent discount at LensCrafters, mentioned above. Sears Optical offers 60 percent off on eye exams ("never more than $45"), 30 percent off on ordinary prescription glasses, and 40 percent off on "Transitions" adaptive lens eyewear.

Other Deals and Discounts

- *AAA discounts.* A few providers offer AAA discounts on eyewear; again, LensCrafters offers a 30 percent discount to AAA cardholders.
- Like dentistry, free and discounted eye care may be available if you have an ophthalmology or optometry school nearby, such as the Meredith W. Morgan Eye Center at the University of California at Berkeley.

Veterinary Care

When people think about health and health care, they don't often include animal care in their thinking. That said, when something does happen to a pet, most people don't think twice about spending money, sometimes a lot of it, to make their beloved pets right. The pet business is lucrative for the vets and suppliers in the business, but it is still very competitive, and lots of deals await patient shoppers.

Free Stuff and Services

As I researched health and health services, it became clear that people can be more sensitive to the needs of animals when their owners are in poverty than to the needs of the owners themselves. There are a surprising number of freebies—mostly veterinary services—available to pet owners.

- *The Humane Society of the United States* (www.humanesociety.org) offers a list of national and state resources, including charities and government programs, to help pet owners in need. These services fund or finance everything from free spaying and neutering to diagnostics and treatment of more serious pet diseases.
- "Helping people and their pets stay together" is the apt slogan of pet retention resource portal Keep Your Pet (www.keepyourpet.com). Their objective is to keep you from surrendering your pet to a shelter; to that end, they offer a list of various pet services, some for free, to help (see the "Veterinary Care Assistance" tab).
- Your own vet may also be inclined to help from time to time, especially if you're a "regular" customer. It never hurts to ask.

Other Discounts and Deals

As stated earlier, the "vet" business is competitive; in addition, there is strong public interest in activities like spaying and neutering, which can result in heavily subsidized pricing. Here are a few examples:

- *The American Society for the Prevention of Cruelty to Animals* (ASPCA), in partnership with PetSmart Charities, offers a list of low-cost spay/neuter programs at www.aspca.org/pet-care/general-pet-care/low-cost-spayneuter-programs.
- As with dental and eye care, it is possible to get reduced-cost or even free pet care from an accredited veterinary college or university. The American Veterinary Medical Association (AVMA) publishes a list of such institutions (see "Veterinary Education" under "Professional Development" at www.avma.org) searchable by state.
- Finally, many pet supplies and medicines are sold online, making them much cheaper to obtain than from a traditional retailer or veterinarian. For meds, check out 1-800-PetMeds or PetCareRx; additionally, deal and discount portals often have coupons and deals on more traditional pet products.

CHAPTER 5

Money for Life

Special Deals on Legal, Tax, and Financial Services

In the last chapter, I began coverage of deals and discounts on professional services in the health and health care universe. While most of us have more encounters with these professions than most others, we do need legal, tax, and banking and financial services from time to time—some, such as banking services, pretty regularly.

While tax services are typically required by most of us once a year, there are also tax breaks worth mentioning, although I will give only a few important ones that seniors tend to overlook since there are so many once you get down into the tax code!

Banks and bank fees, meanwhile, can be silent killers, as the recent Wells Fargo scandal is helping bring to light. Discounts and freebies can help here too, as they can with some of the financial planning services and resources you may have come to use and rely on.

Legal Services

Hopefully most of us don't need legal services too terribly often. But as most know, when the need arises, such services can be fantastically costly, upwards of $400 to $500 per hour in some cases—when all we need is a simple answer to what at least seems like a fairly simple question.

Free Stuff and Services

As expensive as attorneys are, there is an abundance of "free" resources for legal advice and questions. Some involve contact with real people, usually online in a "chat" or in question submittal formats. Other resources include some pretty well laid out question and answer portals, where you can learn a lot—or even just the right questions to ask—by searching and reading up on the topics in question. Of course, "free" advice may not be the best advice, and it stops well short of local representation in court, but it can help you "get smart" and know what to prepare for when you do finally contact a "pay for" attorney.

By way of warning, however, as with most things that are free, there are caveats to searching around for free legal advice. Many of the portals require registration, and you should beware of cookies that may find their way onto your computer. If you click on a section about bankruptcy law, you may start getting some unpleasant ads; if you register and search for bankruptcy services, likewise, Mr. Big Data out there may get the idea you're in financial trouble—and you'll get offers for things you don't want. You might want to use something other than your main default browser to search these services. Too many "free" sites are simply funnels to direct you to pay for attorneys. As always—caveat freebie.

- *FreeAdvice* (www.freeadvice.com) is the best Q&A portal I found. The site is broken down into a "Find Your Legal Answer" and "Get Legal Help" sections. In turn, the Find Your Legal Answer side has well-organized topics, including "Family Law," "Personal Injury Law," "Real

Estate," "Criminal Law," "Drunk Driving," and several others. Articles contained within these topics will answer a lot of questions right off the bat. The "Get Legal Help" subsection has two subsections, one to "Ask a Legal Question," promising responses in a "few days" to "interesting" questions. And if you're willing to pay a modest fee, you can dialog with a real attorney through the chat page.

- *Findlaw.com* also provides an open and easy-to-use portal into free readable legal advice and a system to refer you to proper attorneys in your area. It stops short of specific legal advice tailored to your situation but is useful as it is for what it is.
- *Free legal aid (state and local programs).* It varies by area, but there are a number of government-sponsored legal aid programs that are designed to provide free legal help to low-income residents who meet eligibility requirements. These programs vary and are usually covered by local government or legal aid webpages—the best approach is to search "free legal aid [your county]" or some such.
- *Pro bono services.* Many law firms require their attorneys to serve a certain number of hours for free for their community—often for low-income or senior citizen clients. If you have a case that might be of interest, particularly a complex one, you can look for a pro bono program through the American Bar Association's findlegalhelp.org page or by doing a local search including the words "pro bono."

Senior Discounts

A number of programs, particularly the "free legal aid" programs mentioned above, are set up to help seniors in addition to low-income individuals. In addition:

- Senior citizens law agencies with discounted services are set up in many areas of the country with large and/or economically disadvantaged senior populations; agencies exist to offer free or discounted legal services. In New Mexico, the Senior Citizens Law Office (www.sclonm.org) is staffed by attorneys providing free legal advice and representation for seniors age 60 and over for health care, public benefits (like Medicaid or VA benefits), housing, advance directives, and other fields. Do a search for "senior citizen law discount [your state or county]."
- *The Federal Administration on Aging* (www.aoa.gov) offers an assortment of free and discounted "Title III-B" legal services "targeted to older individuals in social and economic need."
- *The Council on Aging* is a partially government-funding entity offering a host of services to seniors in many but not all geographies, most recognizably, Meals on Wheels. They also offer discount legal services mainly in the areas of estate planning, trust administration, and elder law. Check with one in your area by searching "Council on Aging [your county]."

Other Deals and Discounts

While there are fairly abundant freebies in the legal space, the profession has mixed feelings about offering deals and discounts to the population at large. The American Bar Association frowns on attorneys offering coupons and discounts through Groupon and other sites on "ethical grounds"—and it seems from my research that most attorneys are heeding this advice. A recent Groupon search retrieved coupon deals on will preparation packages but not legal services per se.

However, there are a few ways to get legal advice that won't bust your budget:

- *Just Answer* (www.justanswer.com) is reachable through FreeAdvice as mentioned above but also exists as a standalone page. A team of lawyers and other experts hang out online to answer any question you might throw their way. After registering with the site (a minor cost) and furnishing a deposit (another cost) you can "name your price" to talk to an attorney through real time chat—they claim most responses in seven minutes or less with "100% satisfaction guaranteed." Prices are a well-kept secret but appear to be mostly in the range of $5 to $15 per question. The site covers not only legal questions but also has doctors, mechanics, accountants, and other experts and is set up to operate 24/7.
- *Employer legal services.* If you work for a large enterprise, chances are you may have some discounted legal services already available—either for free as a benefit or as a benefit you might elect to pay a monthly fee for. These services usually cover routine family law, estate planning, real estate, and other major individual areas; they typically do not cover a home business operated by an employee. The upshot is, if you have a legal problem and are employed by an enterprise, check first to see if you have such a service available.
- *Discount legal plans.* Similar to the contracted "discount dental plans" noted in Chapter 4, you can purchase a deal that affords issue by issue legal advice for $17.95 per month for an individual from Legal Shield (www.legalshield.com). Supplements for trial defense or home businesses are available for $9.95/month. "Worry less, live more" is their apt slogan.

Tax Services

The market for tax preparation software and services is highly competitive; in addition, the IRS recognizes that if people, especially low-income earners, are to file their taxes promptly and correctly, they need some help. As a consequence, there are a number of free tax filing platforms and assistance channels, as well as discounts available for software and services to do more complex returns.

Free Stuff and Services

- *The IRS Volunteer Income Tax Assistance* (VITA) program offers free tax help for persons earning less than $54,000 or with disabilities or with limited English. IRS-certified volunteers provide free basic return preparation and e-filing for qualified individuals. The IRS has a "VITA Locator Tool" online or you can call 800-906-9887. These sites also have software allowing you to prepare your own tax returns.
- *Free services from tax preparers.* H&R Block offers a free federal online tax filing service, which can be upgraded to take care of more complex homeowners' and investors' needs for $54.99. State returns cost $29.99. Free online tax advice chat is available. The free service is recommended for the first year, then it migrates to a $39.99 "basic" service for returning users; data are stored from the previous returns and simply need to be updated. So under some conditions, it is free; in others, it is still cheaper than using a standalone professional tax prep service. But realize that you must make sure your data are in order to guarantee the outcome.
- *Free tax software portal.* TurboTax offers a free online tax entry, calculator, form prep, and e-file tool. Federal returns are free for 1040A/1040EZ filers; state returns are $29.99.

More complex returns have modest fees—but again far less that a professional tax prep service.

- *Free online preparation.* FreeTaxUSA (www.freetaxusa.com) offers free federal tax preparation tools and software with e-filing ($12.95 for state returns) for those eligible to e-file. It covers more complex returns including small business, investment, K-1 partnerships, and earned income credits. They make their money through state returns, advisory services, and other upgrades.
- *MyFreeTaxes.* United Way operates a free tax prep engine for filers earning less than $62,000 a year. This engine appears in other places, such as Walmart (the program receives support from the Walmart Foundation). Live chat and phone advisory services are available from IRS-certified advisors with software provided by H&R Block. (See www.unitedway.org/myfreetaxes/.)

Senior Discounts

Useful tax advising services for seniors include:

- *IRS Tax Counseling for the Elderly* (TCE) offers free tax help for all taxpayers older than 60, specializing in questions about pensions and retirement plans. Many TCE volunteers provide their services through AARP's Tax Aide program and are located at AARP sites; use the AARP site locator tool or call 888-227-7669.
- *AARP Foundation Tax-Aide.* Basically the same service as TCE described above, AARP offers a free tax assistance service using IRS-certified volunteers. You can submit questions online and receive answers in three to five business days, or you can ask in person at one of 5,000 locations in neighborhood libraries, banks, malls,

and community and senior centers. (See www.aarp.org/money/taxes/info-2004/about_aarp_taxaide.html.)

Give an Old Guy a Break: Tax "Discounts" for Seniors

There are too many tax breaks ("discounts") to name here—they could fill an entire book on their own. But in keeping with highlighting senior discounts separately, I thought I'd share three of the more beneficial and oft-overlooked discounts you might qualify for as a senior:

- Over 65? For being 65, you get an additional standard deduction of $1,550 for unmarried taxpayers and $1,250 for married taxpayers (both spouses must be over 65 and filing jointly.)
- Over 59 ½ and contributing to charity? Do it out of your IRA (if you have enough to fund your retirement anyhow). Why? Because you can do it directly without increasing your Adjusted Gross Income by the amount of the withdrawal, thus staying eligible for other tax breaks.
- Are you 65 (or even 61 or 60 in some states)? You may be eligible for a substantial property tax reduction, especially if you are in a low-income bracket. States and counties have recognized that seniors don't typically send kids to school among other things. You'll have to search your locality or meet with them in person and often file for the exemption before a deadline, but it can be well worth it—up to 50 to even 60 percent savings in some localities. As an example, Washington residents over 61 earning less than $35,000 a year can claim an exemption amounting to 60 percent of assessed value.

Other Deals and Discounts

Most of the deals in this section are aimed at getting you to buy tax software; abundant offers and coupons exist to get a discount on the software (and thus switch, hopefully permanently, to that product, in their thinking). Some recent examples:

- Fidelity, USAA, and others offered their customers $20 discounts on TurboTax software.
- Capital One offered 25 percent off on TurboTax online.
- Several retailers, including Best Buy, Walmart, Amazon, and Staples, offered $15 off on TurboTax Deluxe, no coupon required.
- H&R Block is offering several discounts on software and prep services through RetailMeNot.

Banking and Banking Services

It comes as no surprise that the banking and financial services business is quite competitive. Banks in particular have learned to differentiate their services by offering minor discounts and waivers of fees to get you started. Most of these waivers have terms and conditions—minimum balances, direct deposit, and so on—so read carefully. And I've also found that over time banks can and will change the terms without notifying you.

Free Stuff and Services

Almost every bank and credit union offers something for free—free checking if you maintain a minimum balance, free savings for teens, and so forth. There are too many offers to detail here, and most have contingencies that make them not really "free." At the end of the day, the "game" is to get the myriad fees waived that you might otherwise be charged.

My best advice is to shop and compare your local financial institutions carefully, and make sure you include credit unions in the mix if you can. Some "national" banks and credit unions, like Ally and Alliant, offer better deals on "online only" checking accounts and so on, but you lose the access to local personnel and branches, which can be convenient for resolving problems, depositing large checks, and so forth. I'll share a few examples anyhow:

- *Bank5 Connect* (online) has no fees, gives access to thousands of free ATMs, reimburses up to $15 per month for "fee" ATMs, charges only $15 for overdrafts, and pays 0.76 percent on your funds if you maintain a balance of $100.
- *Golden One* (a California credit union) offers free checking, no service fees, and no required minimum deposit or balance. They offer several "free" programs for students and teens as well, a "premium" checking account earning interest, free bill pay, "Popmoney" person-to-person transfers, and access to 30,000 ATMs with a minimum daily balance of $1,000.
- *FindaBetterBank.* Okay, so the process of sorting through and comparing all the offers is a daunting task? Too much research; too much fine print? Here's a resource to cut to the chase—FindaBetterBank (www.findabetterbank.com) will compare offerings in your zip code after asking a few questions about what services you're looking for. I probably should have started the section with this one!

Senior Discounts

If you search and shop carefully, you'll find enhanced banking service bundles for seniors—and in many cases, "seniors" can be age 55 or even 50:

- *Bank of America* offers an "Advantage for Seniors" account for age 55+ with the usual free features plus interest payments, free checks, preferred interest rates, a free safe deposit box, free cashier's check and travelers check services, and a host of other perks.
- *State of Massachusetts.* A *state* offering senior discounts on banking? Well, not really, but yes, indirectly. By law, state chartered banks must offer seniors over 65 free checking and savings accounts.

Other Deals and Discounts

Other than the above, there is nothing really to highlight here. Shop diligently and carefully, and realize that there may be a cost to switching banks—the fact that I've been a customer of my current bank for 35 years has helped when it comes to resolving problems, getting fees waived, and so forth.

Financial Planning and Investment Services

Like banking, financial planning and investment services can be highly competitive—but unlike banking, there isn't a whole lot they can offer for free. Generally "free" or "discounted" involves some kind of a teaser to get you in the door. Here are a few worth mentioning, and for the rest, a little local research (and a bold request for a discount or freebie when you walk in the door) might help.

Free Stuff and Services

Many financial advisors, like other professionals, will offer a free half hour just to get to know you and have you get to know them and to give them a briefing on your situation. The following offer from the CFP (Certified Financial Planner) Board is worth noting separately:

- *CFP Board Financial Planning Days.* Every October, the CFP Board joins forces with three nonprofits—the Financial Planning Association (FPA), the Foundation for Financial Planning, and the U.S. Conference of Mayors. You get a "no strings attached" consultation with a CFP advisor plus access to classroom workshops. CFPs are trained to look at the big picture holistically—not just investments, but budgeting, credit and debt, taxes, estate planning, insurance, and college and retirement planning. It's a good "free" way to introduce yourself to the financial planning process as well as to get to know an advisor.

Senior Discounts

Surprisingly, given the tendency for seniors to have wealth and need help managing it, there aren't a lot of discounts specifically available to seniors in this category. One worth noting is through AARP:

- *TD Ameritrade Investment Services.* AARP members get up to $1,000 in cash or gift cards and three hundred free trades (for a $250,000 balance; less for smaller amounts, e.g., $300 for $50,000), one year of waived professional management fees, and free education and research resources.

Other Deals and Discounts

Lots of other "deals" may crop up from time to time, mostly as temporary promotions. You probably won't find them in deal or coupon portals but by other promotions (most of us have been invited to nice dinners to see a pitch on investment management, annuities, or some such—that doesn't qualify as a freebie or discount in my book, although the dinners are pretty nice).

The financial planning and investment world is supported by commission sales or fees. Both can eat you up over time if you're not careful; typical fee-based services run 1 percent of the value of assets being managed. That doesn't sound like much, but 1 percent year after year can add up, especially in today's low-return markets, where earning 3 or 4 percent can be a challenge. With that in mind, I'll highlight one "discount" advisory service worth a look:

- *Vanguard Personal Advisor Services.* Though online and not local, Vanguard offers full investing guidance for an annual fee of 0.30 percent, compared to the typical 1 percent, for a minimum investment balance of $50,000. So if you have $300,000 in accounts, including IRAs, your annual fee would be only $900, not $3,000. The downside is that while the advisors can help with investment, tax, and retirement planning issues, they are generally not trained in the areas of insurance or estate planning. You may have to seek these services elsewhere.

And then, of course, there is the following:

- *Discount brokers.* If you manage your own investments, the economy of online and discount brokers is well known and $7.95 trades are easy to find. These fees were once in the hundreds of dollars and in the $30 to $40 range before the widespread advent of the Internet. Look for other services such as investment tools and human advisors, and shop carefully.

CHAPTER 6

Well Dressed, Coiffed, and Fed

Freebies and Discounts on Clothing, Personal Care, and Food

Finally, we get to one of several categories of necessities that is simply too wide to list anywhere near the full range and assortment of available freebies and discounts. The categories of food, clothing, and personal care are extremely well supplied and competitive at the retail level—as you well know as you've probably been clipping "cents off" coupons for years if you're reading this book.

Like I say, I can't list them all. By nature, true freebies can be hard to find—most are merely samples, though there are free food banks for the elderly, low-income, and other disadvantaged groups. Discount offers tend to be temporal (lasting for short time periods) and, for food items, tend to be small. Fifty cents off here, two bucks off there. I will try to describe some of the larger and more "evergreen" discounts, as well as point you to the places where you might most easily cut to the chase for the smaller and more frequent offers for food, clothing, and personal care items.

Food

Let's make a bet. Do a Google search for "free food." How many "results" are returned? Guess the number.

If you guessed 1.45 *billion*—or something close—you win.

Do a search for "free food" or "free food coupons." You get lots of listings here too, many from the coupon sites you've already become familiar with. But to most of them, the phrase "free food coupon" means that you can print a discount coupon "for free"—that is, at no charge. So the food isn't free, the coupon is. Surprise. Search stymied. Or is it?

The vast majority of free food is not really available as take home food products but rather as freebies (and discounts and offers) for food items from restaurants. As I don't consider eating out a "necessity" for most, I will cover restaurant freebies and discounts, including fast food, in Chapter 12 in Part III ("Discretionary/Pleasure").

Free Stuff and Services

In the food-for-home-use product universe, "free stuff" really translates to free samples. Samples can be fun, and you can "subscribe" to sample deliveries in some portals to get yourself on a list for regular sample shipments. These samples will save you some money over time, as well as expand your universe into new and exciting (?) food products. The downsides: you may end up with a lot of stuff you don't want or like, and many free offers will have marketing and personal info strings attached. One site—freesamples.com—simply redirected me to a discount coupon site with required registration—no freebies.

Again, caveat freebie! This may not be everyone's cup of tea, but for modest savings and some adventure, here are a few portals to check out:

- *Free food samples (sites and portals).* There are a lot of sites that claim to offer free food samples—but when you get more involved, they either aren't free (discount coupons) or don't specifically offer food. The best resources I've found include:
    - *Scamfreesamples.com* acts as a portal to other free sample and free sample by mail sites. The scam-free promise is worth paying attention to as well.
    - *Shareyourfreebies.com* is a by-mail and by-coupon site distributing food, personal care, and other freebie samples. You can also sign up for alerts, which give instant access and daily e-mails about product offers as well as local restaurant offers.
    - *Yofreesamples.com* is similar to ShareYourFreebies described above.
- *Food banks.* For low income or people in substance abuse or other treatment programs, an assortment of free food banks are available, usually funded and run by government and/or nonprofit agencies. Search "free food" or "food banks [your city or county]." "Gleaners"—who take damaged items from groceries and other food outlets and make them available to general populations and sometimes seniors ("Senior Gleaners" agencies exist in some locales) also provide a source of high-quality food in amounts greater than the samples mentioned above. Again a local search will bear fruit.

Become a Taste Tester

Food product makers and fast food chains of all sorts do extensive research on new product and ideas, which usually culminates with a real test to see if real people from the real world really like them!

These tests can be conducted anywhere. Many are done in U.S. cities that offer a representative demographic useful for testing—Columbus, Ohio; Minneapolis–St. Paul, Minnesota; and St. Louis, Missouri, are examples. Particularly if you live in one of these cities, you can get free food—and be paid—for testing products and sharing your opinions! And you can do it over and over.

So-called "sensory testing agencies" conduct the tests and recruit (and pay!) people just like you to conduct them! See fpiTesters (www.fpitesters.com) if you live in the Twin Cities or The National Food Lab (www.thenfl.com) if you live in Livermore, California.

Just search for "taste tester [city name]" and you'll run into a few opportunities to taste the latest incarnation of Spring Quinoa or some such.

Senior Discounts

Freebies and discounts on specific food items for seniors are not commonly found. What is fairly common—but not that well known—are senior discounts at grocery stores and chains. Most are offered in the form of senior discount *days*—a discount given on a whole basket on a certain day, usually a less-busy weekday. As you'll see, the definition of "senior" is fairly broad. Some product categories like alcohol and tobacco are excluded. Here are a few examples:

- *A&P Supermarkets*—5 percent discount on Tuesdays for purchases more than $30 to seniors over 55.
- *Bashas Supermarkets* (Arizona)—10 percent off to seniors over 55 for a $15 purchase.
- *Farm Fresh* (Virginia)—5 percent discount on Tuesdays and Thursdays, 55+, no minimum purchase.
- *Fred Meyer* (and Fry's, its corporate sibling)—10 percent discount on first Tuesday of the month and every Tuesday in November and December, 55+, no minimum purchase.
- *Great Valu Foodstores* (mid-Atlantic)—5 percent discount on Tuesdays and Thursdays, 60+.
- *Grocery Outlet*—10 percent discount one or two days a month, varies by store, 60+.
- *Harris Teeter*—5 percent every Thursday, 60+.
- *Hy-Vee*—5 percent, one day each week (varies by location), 55+.
- *Kroger*—10 percent, first Wednesday of each month, select locations, 60+.
- *Meijer*—15 percent off general merchandise once a month, 62+, varies by store.
- *Publix*—5 percent, Wednesdays, 60+.

If your supermarket isn't on this list, simply ask a customer service rep.

Other Discounts and Deals

There are dozens of sites offering printable coupons and coupon codes for mostly small discounts on food items. Like clipped newspaper coupons of old, you can spend a lot of time to achieve relatively small savings, but well organized navigation allows you to get to what you want more quickly. It isn't everyone's cup of tea, but if you work at it regularly, you may be able to save $10 to $15 a week or so on groceries—savings that can add up nicely. Here are a few of the many sites:

- *DealsPlus* (www.dealsplus.com) is one of my favorite deal portals; check out the "Grocery & Food" page under "Deals" (also has vitamins and other health products).
- *Groupon* (www.groupon.com) has numerous (222 on last search) coupons in the food and drink category, including restaurants; these deals are in your area given by your computer's locator. These aren't just "cents-off" deals; many are 40 to 50 percent off.
- *Dailygrocerycoupon.com* distributes hundreds of printable store coupons for not only food but also household cleaning supplies, personal care items, and so on. You can look at coupons by brand or category.
- *shopathome.com* may have the best and most navigable assortment of small-discount printable coupons under its "Grocery" link. You can navigate by typical aisle of the grocery store—coffee and tea, baby food, and cereal, for instance.
- *coolsavings.com* has numerous printable coupon deals with fairly well-organized categories, mostly small discounts in the $1 range.

What about *Healthy* Food?

So far what I've really covered has been mainstream food—"processed" food in the eyes of the more exacting element of the population who seek out purity in organic and non-GMO food products. Since the healthier food products are expensive to begin with, are there freebies, deals, and discounts to be had on the more "progressive" side of the food aisle?

Turns out it indeed is not too hard to find deals, discounts, and even freebies. Organic and other specialty food producers are only all too willing to put their product in people's hands (and stomachs) in the interest of gaining and retaining their interest.

The portal allnaturalsavings.com is the workhorse in this category. They publish a list of "80 Natural and Organic Companies That Will Send Free Stuff" and have an active "freebies" tab. Beyond that, they have a well-organized site full of coupons and online deals.

The portal organicdeals.com is also worth a look—check out the "Grocery" tab, which points you to deals at Whole Foods, Trader Joe's, and Sprouts.

The upshot: you can eat healthy and save too.

Clothing

Free Stuff and Services

I've found over time that not very much clothing (at least in my household) is purchased at full price. The clothing market is extremely crowded, competitive, and full of product rendered obsolete by fashion change or odd colors or simply because someone ran out of one or two of the sizes offered. It doesn't take much skill to ferret out good deals on clothing.

Most do this by retailer—from Abercrombie & Fitch to Macy's to Walmart—so it's retailer ads and coupons you need to watch. More surprisingly, there are a few freebies to be had, and there are web-only discounts and deals, some quite deep, to be had. I'll provide a small sampler.

Want a Dutch Masters T-shirt? Whether you're just looking for a free t-shirt or want to impress your friends with the cheap cigars you smoke—you can get one for free.

- *Freaky Freddies* (www.freakyfreddies.com) has a listing of assorted freebies—mostly socks and t-shirts but also shoe insert samples and other like items. You must stop by to claim your "Big Ass Fans" hat.
- *Tryspree* (www.tryspree.com) also has a listing of free clothes, somewhat more oriented toward samples than Freaky Freddies. You can get a free sample of "Leather Max" industrial working gloves or a free "Don't Drink and Drive" wristband among other things.
- *About Free Stuff* (www.1aboutfreestuff.com) also specializes in free clothing again in more of a free samples format. Several lines of athletic socks offer freebies to try out for size.

Senior Discounts

Senior discounts tend to run by retailer, not by clothing items or clothing companies per se—and many tend to be special "discount days." Here are a few for major clothing retailers:

- *Dress Barn*—10 percent off on Tuesdays and Wednesdays, 62+, varies by location.
- *Kohl's*—15 percent off on Wednesdays (55+)—this is one of the better senior deals out there.
- *Bon-Ton Department Stores*—10 to 15 percent off on senior discount days—as noted in newsletters and e-mails.

- *Banana Republic*—10 percent off (62+).
- *Peebles Department Stores* (including Palais Royal and Stage stores)—15 percent, first Tuesday every month (50+).

Other Discounts and Deals

- *DealNews* (www.dealnews.com) has a whole tab devoted to discounted clothing items and shoes. Many are through manufacturer outlets, so you usually get the best possible pricing—recently select North Face clothing was being sold at 50 to 70 percent off, with free shipping on orders more than $50.
- *BeFrugal.com* offers deals for select retailers of men's and women's apparel—for example, Gap, Banana Republic, Eddie Bauer, Brooks Brothers, Macy's, and Lord & Taylor. Most are 3 to 6 percent off general merchandise—not just closeouts.
- *RetailMeNot* offers deals from clothing retailers, some of which might be found elsewhere but tend to be for higher-end retailers like Lands' End, H&M, L. L. Bean, Ralph Lauren, Victoria's Secret, and others. In some cases I saw the same deals on the purveyor's own "sale" site.

There are many, many more deals and discounts, so my advice is to pick a few portals, do searches for what you're looking for, and surprise yourself.

Personal Care

The "personal care" category is a loosely defined aggregate of products and services, including everything from cosmetics to haircuts to weight loss to spa services to health aids such as vitamins and vitamin supplements. I can't cover it all here, but the industry is highly competitive with marketers, large and small, vying for your attention and to get you to try something. As a result, there are abundant freebies and deals if you know where to look.

Free Stuff and Services

- *Volunteer your hair*. Free salon services, mainly for hair, may be available from the many trainees and apprentices who are actively honing their skills to get into the profession. For the cost of a signup, you can find out about "75 to 100 percent discounts" for "volunteers" at Salon Apprentice (www.salonapprentice.com). (Yes, there's a website for everything, isn't there?!) You can also search for "free beauty services [your city]" to locate similar opportunities, many at local cosmetology schools.
- *Free samples*. Marketers have found that free samples are a good way to get people started on personal care products, and there are several good "free" portals with rich assortments and regular updates. Sample Buddy (www.samplebuddy.com/free-personal-care-samples) is one of the best and easiest to use portals to regularly receive free sample offers. Free! Mania (www.freemania.net/samples/cosmetic.htm) is another site with a good selection of free personal care products.
- *Free weight-loss plans*. You can spend hundreds to get a tailored diet and weight-loss plan—but before you do, there are several "free" regimens online. Some are "fronts" to get you started and try a product or program, but they appear to be worth a try before you invest real money. Some, like MyFitnessPal.com, offer a free app for calorie counting and/or fitness tracking. Check out The Lose Weight Diet (www.theloseweightdiet.com) or do a search for "free weight loss."

Senior Discounts

There aren't many personal care discounts aimed directly at seniors, but I found a few:

- *Great Clips*—$3 discount to customers 60 and over.
- *MasterCuts*—20 percent discount on salon care services and products for 60, Monday through Thursday only.
- *Avon Products*—20 percent discount on all products from the website (50+) if you're a member of seniordiscounts .com.
- *Walgreens*—20 percent off on Seniors Days for those 55+ and AARP members if you're a "Balance Rewards" member. There are lots of personal care products at Walgreens, and other similar stores have similar deals.

As always, a search for "senior discounts personal care" will get you going.

Other Deals and Discounts

The competitive nature of the personal care industry brings ample deals, many of which are available through your favorite deal portal. Some portals have more and better deals than others:

- *Groupon.* At last count, Groupon had 499 deals on their "Beauty and Spas" page, a little more than 10 percent of *all* the deals they had going that day. Groupon does a nice job of presenting deals in your area—57 percent off on a shellac or manicure in "midtown" of my city was the "headline" deal on the day I checked. It's also easy to search by the type of service you're looking for.
- *Amazon.com.* We all saw this coming—online retail heavyweight Amazon is out to kill categories like books,

music, videos, and electronics—and now clothing and personal care. A trip to Amazon's "Health and Personal Care" department gives hundreds of well-organized deals with deep discounts and coupons for cosmetics and health products, including vitamin supplements and home care products. Particularly if you're a "Prime" member ($99 per year gives free two-day shipping and other perks), this starts to become pretty attractive—and easy.

CHAPTER 7
Getting Around

Auto Maintenance and Repair Freebies and Discounts

Every one of us (i.e., those among us who own a car or truck) dreads the unavoidable and always unexpected car repair, which can be one of the biggest budget busters of our time. But there are ways to (1) get some of the little stuff done free, (2) get ahead of some of the big stuff so it is less expensive, and (3) get some deals and discounts to make it all go down a little better.

The free stuff can cover some small but commonly annoying situations like installing windshield wipers or plugging a tire that picked up a nail or screw. It can also help with preventative maintenance—fluid checks, brake checks, and so on to keep you going more safely and avoid more damaging breakdowns. Not surprisingly, the free stuff—like most free stuff—is designed to get you into the store or shop—but in my experience, most of these shops are honest and will not deceive you to gain your business.

Free Stuff and Services

- *Free check engine light diagnosis*. O'Reilly Auto Parts, AutoZone, and Pep Boys are auto parts stores that offer free diagnostic testing on check engine lights (sometimes called "code retrieval"). These three national chains have retail locations all over the country.

- *Free oil and battery recycling.* Advance Auto Parts, AutoZone, O'Reilly, Pep Boys, and others will recycle your used motor oil and other fluids, batteries, and more (unless locally prohibited by law)—whether or not you buy replacement in their stores.
- *Free battery check and installation.* AutoZone, O'Reilly, Pep Boys, and Advance Auto Parts will check your battery for free. Advance Auto Parts will also install a new battery for free—you just buy the battery.
- *Free alignment check.* Proper wheel alignment makes for a smoother ride and better and more even tire wear. Pep Boys, Goodyear, Les Schwab, and others offer free alignment checks.
- *Free flat tire repair.* Got a nail in your tire? Les Schwab, Goodyear, Costco, America's Tire, and others will fix it for exactly nothing—and in a jiffy—if it's in the main road contact surface and tire belt.
- *Free auto service manuals.* Repair and service manuals for most vehicles as well as ATVs and other items are available for PDF download. Check out free-auto-repair-manuals.com or www.autoeducation.com.
- *Free windshield wiper installation.* Anybody can buy new windshield wipers; it's not that hard. But installing them—especially when it's raining outside and you're in a hurry—is a whole other matter. Pep Boys, AutoZone, O'Reilly, Advance Auto Services, and others will do it for free.
- *Free windshield repair.* Depending on your auto insurance and its glass coverage features, you can often get cracked

or starred windshields repaired and sometimes replaced with zero out of pocket. Insurance companies generally want you to replace your windshield for safety reasons and tend to look the other way when local auto glass repair shops and portable technicians bill the insurer an amount that covers your deductible. These are mostly local companies—search "free windshield repair" in your area.

- *Free brake inspection.* Brake wear can creep up on you, first compromising your stopping experience, then causing damage as metal rivets on your brake pads or shoes come in direct contact with your drums and rotors. Scratch these up enough and the cost of the brake job goes up dramatically. Firestone, Pep Boys, Goodyear, and others offer free brake inspections, which may cover other aspects of the vehicle as well.

Senior Discounts

Senior discounts are not widespread at least in the national auto parts and service chains. However there are many available in smaller, local "mom-and-pop" auto service locations, typically in the 10 percent range and typically for the 55 to 65 and older age group. By way of example, Sun Devil Auto, a chain of twenty service shops in the Phoenix, Arizona, area, gives varying discounts to seniors over 60. Some of the major service oil change chains—Jiffy Lube, Valvoline, and others—are also known to offer a 10 percent discount.

Bottom line—as with all senior discounts—it's worth the time to search, and it never hurts to ask.

Other Deals and Discounts

Most of the major chains make regular coupon offers—so many it's hard to keep track of them all. Many of them are offered through the major "deal" portals—Groupon, DealsPlus, Deal-News, RetailMeNot—and if you're looking for a particular type of service or product, such as Firestone Tires, you can often go to their website or search "Firestone deals discounts" to get to their deals page (www.firestonecompleteautocare.com/offers/). Getting on their mailing list or joining their club or loyalty program will also help, but you can get buried in offers for something you might need only once in a while. Some retailers like Advance Auto Parts offer discounts for online purchases more than a certain amount.

CHAPTER 8

Home Sweet Home

Home, Home Maintenance, and Home Improvement Freebies and Discounts

Home ownership may be wonderful, but it comes with a long laundry list of maintenance items, all of which can drain your budget rather quickly. And if you decide to improve the home, the expenses can really start adding up.

Like most other industries I'm covering in this book, the home maintenance and improvement industries are highly competitive and dominated by relatively small and local suppliers and contractors. The services also tend to be rather expensive; there are few equivalents to changing oil or windshield wipers on a car. As such there are few freebies but an abundance of deals and discounts in this space.

I will cover routine home maintenance, home cleaning, pest control, yard maintenance, security services, yard maintenance, and home improvement services in this chapter.

Free Stuff and Services

As home maintenance and improvement services tend to be relatively big ticket items with relatively small providers, there aren't many freebies in this arena. The main freebie of any use comes in the form of software and apps.

- *Free software and apps.* There are a number of free apps and software packages to help you manage your home or multiple homes if you're a landlord or vacation home owner. BrightNest (www.brightnest.com) turns your home into a project and helps you maintain and manage it with customized task lists, alerts, savings and maintenance goals, and more. You can also access thousands of different sets of DIY instructions for various home maintenance tasks—each of which can save you money. HomeZada (www.homezada.com/mobile-apps.html) allows you to inventory everything in your home, including copies of warranties and receipts, track maintenance contracts and intervals with alerts, and does it all for multiple properties, handy if you're a real estate baron. iFixIt (www.ifixit.com) is a user community–supported DIY home repair and improvement manual.

Senior Discounts

So far as home cleaning and maintenance services go, given the relatively high level of home ownership for seniors, there were surprisingly few discounts aimed directly at seniors. The upshot seems to be that seniors will get the same discounts as everyone else—see the next section. But there are a couple of notable services, some subsidized, made available to seniors recognizing their challenges in maintaining their homes. As is always the case, particularly with senior discounts and particularly given the "local" nature of most of these providers, you should get in the habit of asking for the senior discount.

- *Senior home repair programs.* Various federal, state, and local agencies have recognized that while senior home ownership rates are high, their ability to maintain and repair their homes may be impaired, especially if they're in a low-income situation. The federal Very Low-Income Housing Repair Program can give grants up to $7,500 and loans up to $20,000 for qualifying seniors age 62+. Search "senior home repair programs [your area]."
- *Synergy Home Care* offers a "Light Housekeeping" service targeted to seniors and disabled residents. The service isn't a full housecleaning but rather an "assist"—they work alongside you as needed. They also do lawn and garden work, all for a cost less than a full service housecleaning (www.synergyhomecare.com). SeniorsforSeniors, a Canadian enterprise, is another example, and I expect this idea to catch on as more of us get older.
- A few lawn and garden maintenance providers offer a 10 percent senior discount. On a national level, Scotts Lawn Care and TruGreen Lawn Care offer this discount, but it isn't consistent at all locations.
- Like a regular display of flowers in the home? Like to give them as gifts? 1-800-Flowers.com and FTD.com offer 15 percent discounts to 50+, and lots of local florists offer similar discounts to this lucrative market.

Other Deals and Discounts

Freebies? Hardly any. Senior discounts? Few and far between. Where it really gets interesting, given the number of providers in the home space, is the "other deals and discounts" category, where there are plenty. Naturally, for any service or improvement you seek, it's worth searching the standard deal portals and online using a search engine qualified with you location.

Occasionally you might find veterans and military discounts too. But the best deals I found were consistently through Groupon:

- *Groupon.* It appears that the eight-hundred-pound gorilla for discounts in the home space, like other categories, is Groupon (www.groupon.com). The "Home Services" link points you to 119 services—not a huge number considering the 5,000 or so entries on a given day. But the discounts are deep, especially for first-time services—50 to 75 percent off for floor and carpet cleaning, garage door tune-ups, pest control services, window cleaning, moving services, lawn maintenance, dryer vent cleaning, sewing machine or vacuum repair, appliance repair, and so on—this list was long, and the deals were attractive and presented for each local area.

  Somewhat surprisingly, competitors DealsPlus and DealNews and others had home and garden deals—but none of them were about services, only discounts on products, mostly through major retailers—so if you're looking for patio furniture, home and garden tools, and the like, these portals are worth a stop.
- *Home cleaning services.* Most, if not all, home cleaning services—Molly Maid, SunnyMaids, MerryMaids, and others—offer a deeply discounted first visit or two to get you started. These are national franchisors with local franchisees that will often make their own offers. Molly Maids recently offered $45 off on the first cleaning; SunnyMaids offered a three-hour cleaning for $52.50 (similar discount), and MerryMaids offered $100 off the first five cleanings.
- Yard and landscaping services tend to work like home cleaning services—most offer initial discounts to get you

started although not as deep as the home cleaning services. TruGreen Lawn Care, a national chain, offered a $29.95 first application and lawn care analysis—a good deal but the grass may be greener elsewhere.

- The home security business is extremely competitive; the products and services also carry a high margin. Like other home services, there is a tendency to offer fairly large teasers to get you to install a system, then of course they make it up on the "backside" with your regular monthly payments for monitoring and so forth. The discounts are often designed to get the salesperson in the door. Many of the national providers like ADT are sold locally through local dealers, so it's difficult to pin down any consistent discount or discount policy. As usual, I recommend a local search, and in this case, a careful analysis of the discount to see if it is really cheaper than the next competitor or a simple "markup-markdown" scenario.
- Finally we arrive at home improvement, a subcategory in which you're far more likely to buy a product than a service, although services in the forms of construction and remodeling are prevalent too. Here is where the deal portals like DealNews, DealsPlus, and a few others, such as Slickdeals (www.slickdeals.net), can come in handy.

Slickdeals broadens the home and home-improvement category into ten subcategories, including "Appliances," "Bed & Bath," "Crafts," "Furniture," "Gardening & Outdoor," "Home Decor," "Kitchenware & Cookware," "Lighting," "Storage & Cleaning," and "Tools." The deals were numerous and compelling and delivered through major retailers who likely offered the same deals on their sites. But it was nice to see dozens of good deals for lighting from Amazon, Staples, Costco, Home Depot, Walmart,

Best Buy, and others all in the same pages—so next time you need an LED light bulb or two, Slickdeals is a good place to go. Ditto for "Furniture," which breaks down into eight subcategories, and the other major "Home" categories are covered by this site.

- *Overstock.com.* I haven't mentioned this large deep-discount online retailer yet in this narrative, although I know it has a good following. But here, in the home improvement category, it shouts out to me. Whereas the other sites have standalone merchandise and "finished" goods for home and home improvement, Overstock has a good selection of the piece parts that get built into—and inside of—a good-sized home improvement project. They have a good selection of bath and kitchen hardware, rough and finish plumbing, rough and finish electrical, tile and tiling supplies, and deep subcategory items such as thermostats, home surveillance, switch plate covers, and the like. The deals aren't huge in some cases, but it's a good one-stop shop for a lot of project needs, particularly if you know what you're looking for. Buyer commentaries about many products also help.

CHAPTER 9

Getting and Staying Connected

Utilities, Communications, and Home Office Freebies and Discounts

Utilities can be a big part of your monthly household budget, and these days, may well be overshadowed by the costs of staying connected—that is, communications and home office expenses to keep in touch in today's digital world.

The rates charged by most utilities are fixed by law, so they don't lend themselves to much discounting or promotional activity. But again in today's modern world, people are finding alternatives to traditional electric service in the form of alternative energy—mainly solar—and there are discounts galore in that competitive field.

Likewise, firms fight over your mobile connectivity; ample discounts exist there, and when I speak of home office products, it's hard to ignore computers and other technology devices. With the exception of utilities, discounts are deep and wide in the competitive arenas covered by this chapter. Freebies, on the other hand, are relatively uncommon with the possible exception of "free" solar panels, which come with strings attached but shouldn't be ignored.

Utilities

The average household spends about $2,500 per year on energy services, and more if you include water, garbage, sewerage, and other services most of us take for granted. As mentioned above, rate regulation and the general noncompetitiveness of these industries leave us with little in the way of discounts and freebies to recognize.

"Freebies" usually are limited to the ubiquitous energy use evaluations designed to help you understand and minimize energy use.

Senior discounts are the main "vein" to probe in this category. A number of utilities across the United States have senior discounts for gas and electric and other utility services. Some have maximum income levels; some are for seniors at any income level, 65 and over and sometimes even 60 and over. While many are modest, usually in the 5 to 10 percent range, some can waive certain charges altogether:

- Many utilities have programs, some with governmental assistance, to provide discounts or free services to customers with special needs. Although they seldom apply to normal seniors with good income, they do help those with disabilities, low incomes, or special medical needs. Qualifying seniors and other can save up to 20 percent on Pacific Gas & Electric rates by enrolling in the California Alternate Rates for Energy (CARE) and can get higher baseline allowances if they have special medical needs. Georgia Power customers can get $18 to $24 off their base electric bill if they are 65+ with a household income less than $23,540.

- The city of Columbus, Ohio, offers a 10 percent discount on electricity for seniors 60 and over with less than $18,497 (single) income and waives water base fees altogether.
- The city of Henderson, Nevada (outside of Las Vegas), waives water and sewer charges for seniors 62+ with qualifying low income.

As with many discounts, a search for "senior discounts [utility name]"—or even a phone call to your local utility—may turn up a modest reward.

Going Solar

The vast and rapidly emerging landscape of solar energy as an alternative to traditional energy sources offers one of the more enticing ways to cut your energy costs—if it makes physical and financial sense. "Physical" sense means you must have a properly located rooftop strong enough to support panels (see Google's free "Project Sunroof" to begin this evaluation for free on your own). Then you must typically contact one of today's myriad solar energy specialists—and endure a sales pitch.

Buyer beware—these systems carry fairly high margins and are often priced to put energy tax credits (which threaten to expire every year but never do—a vital part of the sales pitch) in the seller's pocket, not yours. But the word "free" comes up often in these pitches and so captures the ear of those of us tuned into hearing that word and checking out the details.

"Free" in this case usually means a free evaluation, which can be worthwhile but often is tailored to a seller's product. You'll also hear about "free" solar panels, which of course aren't completely free but come tied to a contract to pay the provider for electricity generated from them.

You provide the rooftop, they provide the panel, and they charge you a usually discounted rate (maybe 20 percent) for the electricity they produce. These deals save you money and get you started with little to no capital outlay and are worth a look—but caveat freebie—check out the details and the reputation of the seller carefully.

Just remember that few things in life are really "free." But "free" can be a good place to start.

Communications Services

Do a search for "free telecom" or "free communications" services and, not surprisingly, you'll come up with very little. The bellwether in this category are the voice over IP (VoIP) services like Skype and Facetime, which, by using the public Internet, are pretty much free and can save you a bundle on long distance, especially international, phone calls (not to mention, you get to see who you are calling in real time.)

But discounts and offers for competitive services such as cellular phones and phone plans run deep and wide. Some are simple discounts; others are tied to the purchase of something else, like a long-term contract, and tend to be very temporal and short term. Each must be evaluated on its own merit. There are senior discounts—although many aren't "pure" discounts but rather state mandated or reduced-service plans tailored to seniors. And there is a deep and wide assortment of discounts and deals available in the highly competitive mobile phone space, too many to give too much detail but I will give a few examples.

Senior Discounts

True senior discounts as percent-off specials on standard services in the competitive telecom space are relatively hard to find. Most are in the mobile phone space, and most discounts come in three basic varieties: AARP discounts, "lifeline" services often mandated by state law and targeted mainly to low-income seniors, and senior "plans," which aren't so much discounts as they are special reduced cell phone packages targeted to senior needs. Some of these may be built around special equipment, like "Jitterbug" phones, aligned to senior abilities and aptitude with technology.

- *AARP discounts.* AARP members can save 10 percent on certain AT&T and Verizon wireless plan charges. Consumer Cellular customers can save 5 percent on regular and reduced-service plans with no activation fees.
- *Lifeline discounts.* For years, telephone service providers have offered, sometimes under state law, discounted lifeline services—a discounted base rate on a single telephone line in a household, targeted to seniors and low-income groups. Normally this wouldn't be of much interest today, but some providers, like Verizon, in some states have extended this concept to cellular service. Search for "lifeline telephone service [your state]."
- *Verizon America's Choice 65 Plus* gives reduced minutes (two hundred) and five hundred night and weekend minutes with voicemail and other features for $29.99 per month. Note that no texting or data service is included;

these plans are not built around smartphones. They are analogous to a smaller "senior portion" available at many restaurants. Many such plans are no-contract, meaning they can be changed as needed if the owner goes on a trip or some such.

- *Jitterbug* prepaid wireless plans offer the simplified Jitterbug handset—really, a regular telephone with large keys on a simple keypad with "senior portion" monthly plans with as little as fifty minutes for $14.99 per month offered in a no-contract format. GreatCall (www.greatcall.com) is one large provider of Jitterbug phones and services.

Other Deals and Discounts

The number, depth, and breadth of discounts in the mobile phone space are staggering and too large to cover here. I will as a consequence focus on *types* of deals and discounts you might look for and find and leave it to your searching skills and capabilities to find the exact deal that suits your needs.

- *Veterans discounts.* AT&T offers a 15 percent military and veteran discount for active-duty and retired personnel. Sprint, Cricket, and T-Mobile have followed suit (not uncommon in this business—if you find a discount at one provider, it is usually available at others). MilitaryBenefits (militarybenefits.info/veteran-military-cell-phone-discounts/) offers a handy summary of plans targeted to military and veteran personnel and their families.
- *Student discounts.* They're a little harder to find and often tied to the school or institution you're attending rather than the fact you're a student, but you can drill down to it pretty quickly with an e-mail address (which unfortunately gives them some marketing info). Or to cut to the

chase, just visit a store or call their customer service line. For Verizon, according to one student who researched it, discounts of 6 to 20 percent were available depending on the institution.

- *Corporate or organization discounts.* Again, the major carriers provide discounts to employees and associates of major organizations—but they'll be hard to find and often require you to supply an e-mail address. But the discounts can be substantial and worth asking about; I've seen 25 percent discounts for some corporate employees—well worth inquiring about, but the providers don't make it easy (a good agent, however, will ask who you work for when you set up your plan).

Home Office

With changing work patterns and the ever-increasing needs, we all have to be "always on"—connected to the Internet for business or pleasure or just staying in touch—and more and more of us have a home office to equip and manage. This isn't a huge category, but there are some special discounts and services worth highlighting, especially for seniors. The major subcategory worth a closer peek is computer and Internet services.

Free Stuff and Services

When it comes to computer and Internet services, "caveat freebie" enjoys no finer hour. There are buckets full of free software, computer cleanup and repair programs offered for free, and even "free" versions of big-ticket software packages like Adobe Photoshop. Look out! Free usually isn't completely free, and I've seen cases where computers get completely gummed up by ad servers after downloading something before checking it out. The free stuff you can rely on is from reputable purveyors—major manufacturers and retailers of computer products.

- *Free PC tune-up.* Office Depot, Staples, and others offer perfectly legitimate free tune up services through most of their local outlets. These tune-ups check for viruses, clean up clutter like temp files, and optimize performance, which can make your machine run much better. Of course, these services exist to get you into the store, but it's typically a fair value proposition.
- *Tech Support Guy* (www.techguy.org) provides free computer support services staffed by volunteers and funded by sponsors and donations. They are available 24/7 and support most products and operating systems. The "cost" is a registration; they have more than 750,000 users.
- *Free publishing services.* Everyone has a book to write, and it's likely to be written in that home office most of us have. In today's digital world, if you have a manuscript, it isn't that hard to get it published and distributed for free, especially as an e-book. Light Switch Press (www.lightswitchpress.com) is one such service—they'll take your manuscript and give you the tools to prep it for market (ISBN number acquisition, cover designs, etc.). You put it up for sale on popular outlets (Kindle, Nook, etc.) and they keep part of the proceeds. So it's free to begin with, anyway—"all" you must do is write the book!

Senior Discounts

If you search a bit (or use seniordiscounts.com mentioned below) you'll find a decent assortment of discounts on products and especially services in the computer and Internet space.

Of course, searches for other products (like office furniture) are easily done with the item followed by "senior discounts." There are enough of them out there to make it worth the search.

- *Seniordiscounts.com*. This major senior discounts portal includes many deals on computer products and services under its computers and Internet tab; it is here I found the "Char Wood the Computer Granny" free computer lessons portal (50+) mentioned in Chapter 2.
- *e-Readers*. Amazon offers 10 percent off Kindle e-Readers—including Paperwhite and Fire tablets.
- *Book and learning material discounts*. While most of us under 40 use the Internet to look up answers to nagging tech questions, a lot of seniors still prefer good old-fashioned books. Que Publishing, a major supplier of printed and online computer books (including for smartphones and tablets) makes their products available at 40 percent off for AARP members (www.quepublishing.com/promotions/aarp-members-40-discount-139839).

Other Deals and Discounts

Everyone offers a good deal on a computer. Production costs decline relentlessly as technology makes progress, and competition is fierce. The deals are so numerous and temporal it almost doesn't make sense to go into them here. My search for "computer and home office deals and discounts" yielded 31.8 million results.

Just search for "[product or manufacturer] deals and discounts," and you'll find dozens to choose from. Deal portals like DealsPlus and Groupon also have a lot of worthwhile deals on computers and other electronics.

- *Open box.* One of the best ways to get a good deal on a computer—and many other hard goods like lawnmowers or other electronics products—is to buy an "open box" copy. Open box simply means someone bought it, took it home, and returned it, often very lightly used but used nonetheless, so legally it is considered "used" and cannot be sold as new. In the "old" days these products were sent back to the factory at great expense; today they are more typically refurbished to manufacturer specs at the retailer's service center. These units collect and can be bought for as much as 50 percent off if you're observant in the store (just ask where the open box shelf is). Most are in excellent condition although some may be missing manuals or small peripherals.
- *Techbargains* (www.techbargains.com) is a discount and deal portal dedicated to the tech and home office space. Most of the entries are links to good deals on manufacturer or retailer sites, but it's a good place to start shopping for a variety of technology and electronic products. A "Small Business" tab includes everything from paper shredders to wireless routers and backup services.
- *"Teacher appreciation" discounts.* Marketers like to publicly recognize the hard work of teachers, and they also see that brand names are something students can and will learn subconsciously if they see a brand used over and over. Those two forces come together to produce some decent-sized discounts—Office Depot gives up to 25 percent off to educators during the back-to-school season for "qualifying" purchases.
- *Student discounts.* It works well—maybe even better—on the student side. College students can get $150 off on most computers and $50 off on Microsoft Office

Home and Student at Best Buy. Microsoft itself offers Office 365 Education for free and many other similar deals. Many college bookstores offer student discounts or waive sales taxes. If you're a student (or a teacher) it's always worth asking and usually worth searching.

Part III

Discretionary/ Pleasure

Freebies, Deals, and Discounts for the "Wants" in Life

CHAPTER 10
Getting There

Freebies and Discounts on Air, Rail, Bus, and Rental Cars

Now we move into the "discretionary" section of the book with both feet—to explore the heavily discounted and promoted world of travel. This chapter explores freebies, deals, and discounts for air travel, rail, bus, and rental car operators.

When we talk "discretionary," marketers get that these are dollars, for the most part, that you don't *have* to spend. As such, their job is twofold—first, to entice you to travel in the first place, and second, to have you pick their brand over the other choices. The Southwest ad slogan "you're now free to move about the country" is classic.

As such, deals, discounts, and price changes occur almost daily and are easy to find, almost *too* easy. Marketers got smart about 40 years ago and started to try to build loyalty and repeat business, not just price competition. You see that result in the ubiquitous loyalty programs out there, which you get your arm twisted to join the first time you purchase a ticket or rent a car.

As covered next, loyalty programs are where most of the freebies are found—although it's a stretch of the definition of "freebie." And they've become an important, but not the only, vehicle for dispensing deals and offers. But on that front, they're not the only game in town; in this chapter, I'll cover the deals and discounts available without committing to a loyalty program.

Loyalty Programs—the Travel "Standard"

In general, most travel operators offer the majority of their freebies and many of their perks and discounts through their membership based loyalty programs. Originating in the travel industry, these programs largely offer the same benefits—not surprising as this industry is ultracompetitive and tends to breed matching values for customers and also not surprising as most of these programs are outsourced to the same handful of agencies that specialize in operating loyalty programs.

Most loyalty programs offer miles or points for paid travel and can be used for more travel, upgrades, or purchases and services outside the mainstream business. Miles or points can be acquired from other sources, such as linked or branded credit cards (e.g., Southwest Visa). You can decide whether these are really "free"—but most programs offer good value once you accumulate enough mileage or points.

I won't compare transport operator loyalty programs here. First, they are quite similar and familiar. Second, they are easily investigated on operator websites. Third, it would bog this chapter and the book down with too much detail.

Air Travel

Despite the fact that airlines have consolidated into five or six major national operators, the business remains ultracompetitive. If you're an airline, it's hard to differentiate your flight from

Chicago to New York. You can try giving out Oreo cookies instead of peanuts, but cost constraints prohibit you from doing more and the main thing the customer wants is simply to get to New York safely, on time, and in reasonable comfort.

Yet if you're an airline marketer constrained by cost to compete on price, you need some other kind of offer. In general, this has turned into the all-encompassing loyalty program—fly with us, and you'll get some points. Fly with us *again*, and you'll get more points and eventually a free trip and other perks. Sure, if you're going to fly an airline more than once, it's worth signing up. It's free save for the fact you'll get lots of e-mails and other offers easily ignored.

But there are other freebies, deals, and discounts worth noting, many of which are pretty well hidden and surprising. I'll get to that now.

Free Stuff and Services

Earn enough miles, and you get a free flight. We all know about that one, but you have to buy a lot of tickets to get there. When you do finally get there, it feels like it's free—especially if someone else, like your employer, paid for the enabling tickets. So I'll acknowledge those free tickets—a little reluctantly—as freebies!

But here are a few more, some out of the mainstream and often overlooked:

- *Airline job for close family member*. Want to travel the world? For free? Simply have a close family member get a job with an airline. Close family member? It varies some by airline, but spouse, parent, child, and sometimes siblings qualify. You fly standby, which can bring some hardships, but for the most part, it works! You might even end up flying first class! Schoolteacher Linda Katz of Grass

Valley, California, spent most of her summer break traveling Costa Rica, New York, Spain, and Puerto Rico for about $200 in government fees because her daughter works for a major airline.

- *Babies and toddlers.* Fairly well known to those who have them, most seats on domestic flights come free for a child under two who will presumably sit on a parent's lap. It works well if there are empty seats on the plane. What's less well known is that on most international flights you can buy the seat next to you at a discount, typically 25 percent off the adult's fare. That might well spell relief for an international passenger parent with a lap child on an eight-hour flight!
- *Military.* As we'll see shortly, discounts for active and retired military and their families are abundant but not so easy to find. But less well known is a program operated by the Department of Defense called "Space-A," or "space available." The DoD uses military or commercially contracted aircraft to fly between military bases in the United States and around the world. By following some relatively complex rules you—and sometimes your family—can "fill" available spaces and fly free or nearly free. (See www.spacea.net.)
- *Cancer patients.* Regrettably, people in dire straits sometimes must travel for treatment, and some carriers have acted to make it as painless as possible. Southwest Airlines offers a Medical Transportation Grant Program to ninety hospitals and institutions nationwide. You may qualify for reimbursement from this program or others from the institution—talk to the travel concierge. Perhaps better yet, the Corporate Angel Network (www.corporateangelnetwork.org) finds empty seats on

corporate jets—and has done so some 50,000 times in 35 years.

- *Get bumped.* This one isn't particularly reliable, and as airlines have become more efficient with their reservation systems, it doesn't happen as often. But with today's fewer and more crowded flights, it's on the upswing again—a flight is overbooked (oversold) and the airline must find volunteers to not fly. The compensation varies by how desperate they are to unfill the plane, but you can get a voucher worth a few hundred dollars typically. You can improve your chances by (1) flying the last flight of the day on a busy lane on a busy day, such as a Monday, Friday, or Sunday; (2) not checking your bag; and (3) staying flexible with your ground transport plans.
- *Complain effectively.* Did the airline misconnect? Run out of peanuts? Lose your bag? Inconvenience you in some other way? You can complain, and it just might get you a flight voucher. Send a polite, concise, not-too-personal, and not angry e-mail to the airline's customer service department. Don't threaten to never fly them again, but rather let them know you're a loyal customer who ordinarily likes to do business with them. Play nice.

Senior Discounts

Most domestic airlines offer some form or fashion of senior discount. Compared to other senior discounts in other industries, they are relatively inconsistent (actual discount and available routes vary) and can be hard to obtain online (you have to call). Worst of all, you can often do better than the senior discounted price by shopping fares carefully. Still, they're good to know about, especially if your situation boxes you into buying an otherwise full-fare ticket.

Many international airlines offer senior discounts—but often only for travel within their home country. Smaller airlines have gotten away from discounts: Alaska once offered 10 percent to those 62 and over; Frontier and JetBlue offer none, citing that "their fares are low enough already." AARP discounts are temporal and typically combined with package tour deals but may be worth a look.

Generally speaking the only way to get a senior discount is to book by phone. A discount may be applied if enough seats are available on a particular flight and you're over 65. The discount varies but is far less than the discount available for advance booking, but it can come in handy if you're forced to pay an otherwise full fare due to short notice or sold-out "cheap" fares—a senior discount can be a last resort.

Other Deals and Discounts

As mentioned at the outset, due to competition, seasonal travel patterns, and short-term "inventory considerations"—availability of unsold seats—there are too many airline deals and discounts at any given time to even try to list. The best approach is to go to an airline's website—there's almost always a "special offers" or "flight deals" or "today's specials" page linked right to the main page. It's fun to shop, especially if you're not fixed into a particular destination or timeframe!

Most airlines have special discounts for targeted groups in addition to numerous temporal deals that pop up on the "deals" page and elsewhere. Some categories of discounts, like student discounts, are not made very public; like senior discounts, you must talk to an agent to see if they apply to that flight that day. Some discounts are only offered on tickets sold through agencies or on package "vacation" deals, not individual airfares. Important deals and discounts include:

- *Advance purchase.* In my book, the best airline deals and discounts still involve buying tickets in advance. Time was once when you had to book two weeks in advance, it had to be a round trip, and it had to involve a Saturday night stay. No longer. While most advance purchases still require a fourteen-day advance period, many today do not; some can be had in seven or even five days. And you don't have to stay the Saturday or book a round trip—with most carriers anyhow. It's still the best way to save 50 or even 70 percent off the full fare.
- *Coupon portals.* For the most part, coupon portals don't offer "pure" savings on airline tickets but instead carry offers for vacation packages, many offered through the major airlines. If you're looking for a weekend getaway, check your favorite deal portal.
- *Air travel portals.* Most of you are familiar with the major travel portals—Expedia, Hotwire, Travelocity, and the like. There are also a few portals that specialize in the air travel portion of your trip, guarantee lowest fares, and occasionally offer their own discounts across the board and to special groups like military. Priceline (www.priceline.com) has been the "killer app" in this category with their "name your own price" platform, but as of September 2016, they have ended that service ("too cumbersome") in favor of deeply discounted "express" fares saving 30 to 40 percent and especially well-suited to last minute travelers. Sites like CheapOair.com, smartfares.com, or Insanelycheapflights.com are also worth a look, especially if you fly a lot and/or are traveling at the last minute.
- *Category discounts.* Like senior discounts, some discounts may be available for military and government personnel, students, children under 21, teachers, and for medical or

bereavement situations. Airlines have moved away from these discounts in favor of lowering fares, especially for advance purchase, across the board. Like senior discounts again, the best approach is to call the airline and be prepared to discuss a particular route and date—but the discount varies, and don't expect it to be better than the lowest published "saver" fare. Once again, they work best in last-minute situations where you might otherwise pay a full fare. For some discounts like military, it may help to check out the air travel portals, including one set up especially for military personnel—www.militaryfares.com.

Rail and Bus

For a variety of reasons, many of us still prefer land-based transportation to air travel. Unlike air travel, there is really only one game in town for U.S. rail passenger travel—Amtrak. But they know that competition is fierce too—it just isn't on the rails. Likewise, there are only a few players in the intercity bus industry—but they have become savvy to competition and to targeted groups of citizens like seniors and military. Here is a short summary of available freebies, deals, and discounts by carrier:

- *Amtrak* offers a good assortment of discounts, but like the airlines, the "saver" fare may be a better deal if available. Also, the discounts don't apply to the relatively more expensive sleeping "accommodations." See www.amtrak.com/discount-train-fares-for-kids-seniors-military-students-and-more. (Kudos to Amtrak for making these discounts transparent.)
    - *Senior discount*—15 percent to seniors 62 and over.
    - *AAA discount*—10 percent for fares, with half off for children ages 2–12, but again it does not apply to saver

fares, and in some lanes, it must be booked three days in advance.

- ◦ *Students*—15 percent.
- ◦ *Disabled*—15 percent for traveler and one companion.
- ◦ *Military personnel and families*—10 percent.
- ◦ *Veterans*—15 percent with Veterans Advantage VetReward card (not a credit card).
- ◦ *Government employees*—special fares on Northeast Corridor trains.
- ◦ *National Association of Rail Passengers members*—10 percent.
- ◦ *Specials*—called "promo codes" for particular lanes at particular times—search "Amtrak promo codes."

- *Greyhound*. The eight-hundred-pound gorilla in the bus industry, like Amtrak, has made their deals and discounts easy to find (www.greyhound.com/en/help-and-info/ticket-info/discounts) and they are worth keeping track of:
  - ◦ *Students*—20 percent (and 40 percent off shipping) with a Student Advantage Discount Card.
  - ◦ *Military and veterans*—10 percent off full price tickets for member and family, 20 percent off for veterans with Veterans Advantage card.
  - ◦ *Seniors*—5 percent for 62+.
  - ◦ *Midweek savings*—up to 40 percent for Tuesday and Wednesday travel.
- *Discount portal*. The portal GoToBus (www.gotobus.com/deals/) offers lane-specific deals and coupons in much the same manner as the air travel portals mentioned above. CheckMyBus (www.checkmybus.com) is another.
- *Megabus*. Upstart discount competitor Megabus (www.megabus.com) offers a very low-cost, low-frills alternative mainly in the eastern half of the United States and the

West Coast. No published discounts, but fares are routinely under $10 and as low as $2.

Rental Cars

The rental car industry, like others in travel, has a largely undifferentiated product and periodic surpluses in low-travel seasons, thus it is very competitive and has recognized certain "target" groups for discounts, such as seniors and AARP members. Loyalty programs are also in full force here and are the source of most freebies and many deals and discounts.

Free Stuff and Services

Outside of loyalty programs, rental car companies don't offer much for free. But there are ways to get some free benefits if you're inquisitive:

- *Class upgrades.* On a budget but driving around a group or family of five? Okay, rent that subcompact at a cheap rate, and if you have to squeeze everyone in, so be it. But upon arrival, it's worth asking for an upgrade to full size or some such—and you'll often get it for free or nearly so. Why? Because everyone wants to rent the small cars because they're cheap! Rental car companies tend to run out of them first and are only too happy to land you in a Chevy Impala or even an SUV at the subcompact rate—just to get them on the road and save the subs for other renters.
- *Free insurance.* When you rent your car, you're often confronted with scary sales pitches for insurance for the rental vehicle. "Why, if you have an accident, perhaps your auto policy covers injuries and damage, but you'll be charged for every day the vehicle is out of service for us, which could be weeks! So here's peace of mind for $15 a day." $15 per day? That's $5,475 a year if my calculations are right—the most

expensive insurance you'll ever buy and a major profit center for the car rental company. Solution? Perhaps your own auto insurance (check it out) or loss damage waiver protection provided by your credit card (many do, check this out too).

Senior Discounts

Seniors are a favorite target group for car rental companies—they are loyal, careful, and tend not to drive that far. Unlike airlines, car rental companies have made the discounts fairly permanent and transparent. Kudos to Budget for not only giving a healthy discount but also throwing in some things many seniors really need—GPS, additional driver fee waived, and a damage limitation.

Company	Type of discount	Amount	Age	Comments
Alamo	AARP	Up to 25%	AARP	"SeniorCircle" membership program discounts also available
Avis	Senior	10%	50+	Leisure rates
Budget	AARP	10 to 25%	AARP	GPS upgrade discount, class upgrade, additional driver fee waived, damage limit
Dollar	Senior	10%	50+	
Enterprise	Senior	Varies	Varies	Varies by location
Hertz	Senior	Up to 25%	50+	"50 Plus" rental program, AARP discounts
National	AARP	Up to 30%	AARP	"SeniorCircle" membership program discounts also available

Other Deals and Discounts

Like many business categories in this space, the competitive nature of car rentals lends itself to scads of short term offers, many of which are handled on the provider's own deal and discount page and most of which can be found on deal and coupon portals. Most car rental companies operate under the franchise model to a degree, and not all franchisees uphold all deals, so you might find some variations within the same company. Here are a few specific things to look for:

- *Car rental portals.* The best deals I've found are at specialty portals like Cheap-Auto-Rentals (www.cheapautorentals .com) and CarRentals.com (www.carrentals.com). These portals post attractive daily deals and can search multiple sites for other deals. Kayak and Priceline offer pretty good deals too. The best deal may not reflect the myriad other fees added—especially for an airport location. Shop carefully.
- *Coupons portals and other coupons.* I've probably seen more coupons for car rentals than any other travel category, anywhere from online to offers enclosed in your Visa bill. Most of these are good but don't beat the least expensive deals you can find in a location with a careful search through a car rental or travel portal. Discounts tend to look attractive and then not work because they're not combinable or don't work at peak times or at all locations.
- *USAA and other affiliations.* A financial services firm aligned to active and retired military personnel, major car rental firms offer good discounts to USAA members. Avis, Hertz, and Budget offer 25 percent discounts, while Enterprise offers 5 percent. As with other offers, "participating locations" applies. Affiliations like this are common

across many service companies, airlines partner up with car rental companies to offer discounts regularly as well.

- *Car rental company discount pages and search.* If you have a favorite car rental company already, all or almost all have a "deals and discounts" page on their own sites, and search also works well ("deals and discounts [company] [location]") too, especially for last minute deals. You may well end up back at a car rental portal with such a search.
- *Pay in advance.* Like hotels covered in the next chapter, some companies are starting to offer good deals for rentals paid in advance (most are paid at the time or return). Budget recently offered an up to 35 percent discount for rentals paid in advance.

CHAPTER 11

Staying There

Hotel and Lodging Freebies and Discounts

Whether you're traveling on business or for pleasure, a vast assortment of hotels and motels await your patronage as you arrive at your home away from home. Most hotels today are branded chains; in fact, most of the familiar chains, like Holiday Inns and DoubleTree are in turn owned by larger hotel conglomerates like International Hotel Group (IHG) and Hilton, respectively.

In this chapter, I will focus on the freebies and discounts offered by the nine largest hotel operators, which in turn account for dozens of familiar hotel brands as just described. I will focus on evergreen freebies and discounts, not the far more numerous special offers one might see for a given geography or time of year.

Since there are so many hotels and so many available discounts and offers—many of them temporary—I will use a slightly different format to capture the complexity and detail of this industry. This is necessarily a small subset of all the available deals. As elsewhere, I seek to "teach you how to fish"—how to find out what's out there easily and quickly yourself.

Loyalty Programs—the Chain Hotel "Standard"

Like other travel operators, most chain hotel operators offer the majority of their freebies, perks, and discounts through their membership-based loyalty programs, most of which are called "rewards" (Hilton Rewards, Choice Rewards, Marriott Rewards, to name a few). Like the transport operators from Chapter 10, these programs largely offer the same benefits, not surprising as this industry is ultracompetitive and tends to breed matching values for customers and also not surprising as most of these programs are run by the same outsourced agencies.

Most loyalty programs offer points for paid stays that then can be used for free nights, upgrades, mobile (app-based) check-in and reservations, special offers, and in some cases, special rates. The biggest "freebie"—if you want to call it that—comes in the form of "free" nights you can accumulate over time—sometimes in substantial numbers with enough paid stays. As with other loyalty programs, the question is whether these are really "free"—but most programs offer good value once you accumulate enough points.

Again, I won't compare loyalty programs. They are familiar, easily researched, often compared, and too lengthy for this book.

Chain Hotel Freebies and Discounts in a Nutshell

Aside from loyalty programs, which only have value for frequent and loyal travelers, there are a few freebies and a fairly wide assortment of discounts that can help even the most infrequent of travelers. And unlike loyalty programs, you don't have to sign up for anything or collect a lot of "paid" stays to benefit. While these discounts are fairly common among the chains, the exact details—like age limits for senior discounts—can vary widely, so I'll present tables describing the discounts.

I found a handful of freebies and six categories of discounts, which I'll present in more detail:

- Senior
- AARP
- AAA
- Government and military
- Advance purchase
- Other

Some of these, like the AAA (American Automobile Association) and other auto clubs, might be quite familiar; others are less so; and all vary a bit from chain to chain.

Freebies and Discounts from Nonchain Hotels

Of course there are many thousands of individual and "boutique" hotel chains across the country; it is too large a task to research and present them all. Mainly, I found that in the absence of loyalty programs (which generally don't make sense for a small singular operation) most gave out freebies and discounts one might normally find in a loyalty program—such as free nights with a paid stay or room upgrades—without the loyalty program overlay.

As an example, the Mauna Lani Hotel and Bungalows (www.maunalani.com) on the Kohala Coast of the "big island" of

Hawaii has no formal loyalty program, although they do keep track of repeat customers and offer special deals, often at check-in, to their loyal customers. They have persistent deals to get a free fifth night stay with four paid nights and/or a breakfast buffet and/or a second adjacent room for families traveling together at half price.

Such freebies and discounts are widely available at nonchain hotels; you just have to look—or sometimes, just ask.

Researching Freebies and Discounts

Especially with the wide ranging field of hotels and hotel operators and the different kinds of freebies and discounts offered, I will "teach you how to fish"—not just give you fish. There are too many "fish" to give within the confines of this section—or even this book—and they change constantly.

To find freebies and discounts, most hotel chains and many individual hotels have special "deals and discounts" or "special offers" web pages. I found that the fastest way to see the most was to enter a hotel chain name (i.e., Hilton) followed by "deals discounts" or some such. This landed me on a page summarizing both the persistent discounts and the temporary offers in an accessible form.

The Nine Major Chains

Here I'll summarize the nine major U.S. hotel chains, many of which of course have international extensions.

Hotel chain	Subbrands	Number of hotels	Deals/discounts page
Best Western		4,100	http://www.bestwestern.com/deals-offers/
Choice Hotels	Comfort Inn, Comfort Suites, Sleep Inn, Quality Inn, Clarion, Mainstay Suites, Suburban, Econolodge, Rodeway Inn	6,300	https://www.choicehotels.com/deals/hotel-discounts
Hilton	Hilton, Conrad, Embassy Suites, Hampton Inns, Hilton Garden Inn, Homewood Suites, Doubletree	4,700	http://www3.hilton.com/en/offers/index.htm
Hyatt	Eleven Hyatt subbrands plus Andaz	600	https://www.hyatt.com/hyatt/specials/offers-landing.jsp
Intercontinental (IHG)	Holiday Inn, Holiday Inn Express, Crowne Plaza, Indigo, Kimpton, Hualuze, Candlewood Suites, Staybridge Suites	5,000	http://www.ihg.com/hotels/us/en/global/deals/hotel-offers

Hotel chain	Subbrands	Number of hotels	Deals/discounts page
La Quinta Inns		800	http://www.lq.com/en/special-deals/special-rate-programs.html?sissr=1
Marriott	Marriott, Courtyard, Renaissance, Residence Inn, Autograph Collection, Fairfield Inn, Springhill Suites, Marriott Vacation Club	4,000	http://www.marriott.com/travel-deals.mi
Motel 6		1,300	https://www.motel6.com/#/home
Wyndham	Wyndham, Days Inn, Super 8, Howard Joÿson, Travelodge, Knights Inn, Microtel, Wingate, Ramada, Baymont	7,800	http://www.wyndham.com/deals-discounts/special-offers/deals-discounts

From here, I'll show some of the persistent freebies and discounts offered by the major US chains.

Freebies

As you might expect with the value of a hotel room and the temptation through abundant loyalty programs to "charge" points for "free stuff," there are few true freebies available. Here are a few I was able to identify, and inevitably even some of them aren't really free—but at least they don't require a loyalty program signup or accumulating points in such a program.

Obviously there are many more such freebies that appear from time to time or are offered by different hotels—this list doesn't cover all.

Hotel chain	Freebie	Qualification	Comments
Best Western	$50 Best Western gift card	Two-night stay	For AAA members only
Choice Hotels	$50 gift card for assorted retailers	Two separate stays	Requires Choice Privileges membership—but not points
Hilton	Family Fun package	One-night stay	Free breakfast for four, premium Internet
	Park, Stay & Go	One-night stay	Free parking at select airports and cruise ports, seven-day parking max

Hotel chain	Freebie	Qualification	Comments
	Stay Hilton, Go Out	One-night stay	Targeted to LGBT community—free beverages, late checkout, free *Out* magazine subscription (digital)
IHG	$25 gas card	Two- (or more) night stays	
Motel 6	Kids stay free	One-night stay	

Senior Discounts

Senior discounts are among the most persistent and often used discounts available. The variation of discounts and especially the qualifying ages among hotel chains is notable. Marriott and Hyatt offer the best rates; Best Western, Choice, and Wyndham have a relatively more lenient definition of "senior."

Generally these discounts and others presented in the rest of this section cannot be combined.

Hotel chain	Amount	Age	Comments
Best Western	10% or more	55+	AARP members also qualify, upgrades, free breakfast
Choice Hotels	10%	60+	AARP members also qualify
Hilton	10%	65+	

Hotel chain	Amount	Age	Comments
Hyatt	Up to 50%	62+	Subject to availability
IHG	Discounted rate	62+	Savings off of best available rate
La Quinta	Varies	65+	Discounted rates vary by location and availability
Marriott	15%+	62+	
Motel 6	10%	AARP	Includes 2 p.m. checkout on request
Wyndham	10%	60+	

AARP Discounts

Closely related—but not exactly identical in most cases—are persistent discounts given to AARP (formerly known as the American Association of Retired Persons) members. One big difference is that there is no minimum age to join AARP, so you can enjoy a "senior-like" discount in your fifties or even earlier (my son got an offer to join when he was eight—true story!). It costs a modest $16 annually to join AARP.

Hotel chain	Amount	Comments
Best Western	10%	"Little extras"—room upgrades, early check in, late checkout
Choice Hotels	10%	Free continental breakfast
Hilton	5%	
La Quinta	10%	
Motel 6	10%	Late checkout
Wyndham	Up to 20%	

AAA Discounts

American Automobile Association (AAA) and other auto club discounts are routinely available to anyone with a membership (age, of course, does not matter). The following five were specifically identified on deals and discounts pages, but I have run into very few hotels that don't give a AAA discount.

Hotel chain	Amount	Comments
Best Western	10% or more	
Choice Hotels	Up to 10%	Participating hotels only
Hilton	5%	
Marriott	15%	Weekends only
Wyndham	10%	

Government and Military Discounts

Here we get into some of the more significant—and varying—persistent discounts you'll find. Most hotel chains have discovered a large, loyal, and frequently traveling base of customers in both the military and in government employment. Most give special discounts or tie rates to the federal government "per diem" allowance so that travelers can use the hotel and not have any leftover out-of-pocket expenses. Some hotels (1) extend these discounts to family, retirees, and/or personal travel and (2) include state and local government employees as well.

Many of these "discounts" are really special rates tied to the federal government's assessment of the cost of living and lodging in an area rather than percentage discounts—hence, they "vary."

Hotel chain	Name of discount	Amount	Comments
Best Western	US government/ military discount	Varies	State/local government too, including government-funded hospital employees
Choice Hotels	Government programs	Varies	Military personnel and family get government rates for personal travel
Hilton	Military family rate	Varies	Special rates include families and retirees
La Quinta	Government discount	Varies	State/local included; rates "at or below federal per diems"
Marriott	Government and military discount	Varies	GSA rates for military, government, state, and local; includes personal travel
Motel 6	"Guests of Honor"	10%	Military, including family and retired
Wyndham	Military appreciation discount	15%	Includes spouses and retired
	Government discount	Varies	Federal per diem rates

Advance Purchase Discounts

Another discount and one of the richest and yet probably unfamiliar to most—although much like the "Wanna Get Away" and other Internet specials offered by Southwest and other airlines—is the advance booking or early purchase discount. Buy (or even just reserve) seven days in advance, and as shown below, substantial discounts are available.

Hotel chain	Name of discount	Amount	Comments
Choice Hotels	"Book Early and Save!"	Up to 20%	Seven days in advance, subject to availability
Hilton	Advance purchase	Up to 20%	Must pay in advance
IHG	"Book Early and Save with Breakfast"	10 to 30%	Includes breakfast
Wyndham	"Book Early"	Up to 20%	Must pay in advance and be Wyndham Rewards member

"Other" Discounts

Best Western "wins" the category of "other" (and more creative!) discounts for special "niche" markets:

Hotel chain	Name of discount	Amount	Comments
Best Western	Online booking rate	Up to 20%	Book online and prepay
	Rider-friendly rate	10%	For motorcyclists; "Ride Rewards" enhanced loyalty program
	Race fan rate	10%	Book with "RaceFan" code
	Business advantage	10%	For small business owners; other perks available
La Quinta Inns	"Bright Now"	10%	For small business owners; other perks available

This list probably just scratches the surface, but it represents what I could find easily as persistent discounts targeted to specific groups.

As you can see from all six of these categories of discounts, hotel chains are getting smart about targeting specific audiences. These freebies and discounts, while quite similar reflecting the competitive environment in this industry, have enough variation to make it interesting. A few tens of percents here and there taken over several trips will save substantial sums for the regular traveler. Shop carefully—and you're likely to find a lot more out there.

CHAPTER 12

Eating There

Freebies and Discounts at Popular Restaurant Chains

America loves to eat out. According to U.S. Department of Agriculture statistics, Americans spend about 10 percent of income on food and about a third of that eating out.

Restaurants, like other "discretionary" indulgences, are large in number and very competitive. To stay competitive, some resort to food quality and ambience to stay ahead of the pack—but most compete on price. And still many more have gotten wise to the idea of diner loyalty and repeat business—so the trick is to get people to come in and try what you have to offer.

That can be difficult because there are so many restaurants out there, so many—probably most—resort to promotions and offers to lure customers in. Anything from one-off coupons and promotions to weekly ads to coupons included in local restaurant guides—anything goes.

Most restaurants have freebies and discounts—teasers to get people in the door and to extend their loyalty. There are simply (far) too many restaurants to capture all the deals available, and

I cannot possibly begin to capture local one-off mom-and-pop operations.

So instead I will offer a listing; a representative sample. A list of the top twenty chain restaurants across the United States, most of which would be described as "fast food." In a possibly refreshing new format, I will summarize freebies, senior discounts, and other deals and discounts in bullet form. These discounts are mostly temporal and are not all-inclusive; they are designed to allow you to "sample the flavor" of what chains have to offer.

I should note that many discounts are not available or are not the same in all locations and that many of them are not found on the company website. And many, *many* more are available through the popular coupon portals, although most of these mimic what's on the company's deal and discount page—if there is one. In some cases, I rely on third-party sources like seniordiscounts.com to capture the discounts for that category.

You'll also find that you'll have to ask for many of the freebies and discounts, especially senior discounts, when you're in the restaurant. Employees usually aren't aware of them or, somewhat cynically, may be trained not to give them unless you ask. As with all discounts, it never hurts to ask.

Clearly this is not intended as an all-inclusive resource but rather as a sample designed to give an idea of what's out there and as a pattern or template to help you discover these deals for yourself. As you might guess, you can search for any restaurant name, then "free" or "senior discount" or "deals and discounts" to find a deal to suit your own personal tastes.

Bon appetite, and dig in . . .

Top 20 Restaurant Chains

(*) not on company website but discovered through third party source.

1. **McDonald's** www.mcdonalds.com/us/en-us/whats-hot.html
    - Freebies: Free app to get access to real time deals.
    - Senior Discount: Free drinks or coffee to age 55+—varies by location and franchisee (*).
    - Other Discounts: Temporary promotions to try new foods, such as Gilroy Garlic Fries on the West Coast.
2. **Subway** www.subway.com/en-us/promotions/sms
    - Freebies: Join the membership program and get a free six-inch sub with the purchase of thirty-ounce drink and get weekly offers and programs on your mobile device.
    - Senior Discount: 10 percent for age 60 and over (*).
    - Student Discount: 10 percent off with a valid student ID (*).
    - Other Discounts: Promotions and offers with registration or mobile app.
3. **Starbucks Coffee** www.starbucks.com
    - Freebies: Join the Starbucks rewards program for a free treat on your birthday, free in-house refills, free drinks every twelve purchases, pay-by-phone, order ahead, and other "perks" (*).
    - Senior Discount: None found.
    - Other Discounts: Temporary promotions through the rewards program, many more on Groupon and other portals; Starbucks discounts are among the more popular items on the independent portals.
4. **Burger King** www.bk.com/offers
    - Freebies: Free Whopper or Original Chicken Sandwich for taking a survey.

- Senior Discount: 10 percent for 60 and over; may vary by location (*).
- Other Discounts: Temporary promotions monthly on "offers" page.

5. **Wendy's** www.wendys.com
    - Freebies: Free Frosties all year by joining MyWendy's program and downloading app.
    - Senior Discount: 10 percent, participation and age limit vary by location (*).
    - Other Discounts: Temporary offers, most on main page.
6. **Taco Bell** www.tacobell.com
    - Freebies: Free add-ons to meals often made available on special days, like free Doritos Locos Tacos on last day of NBA playoffs.
    - Senior Discounts: 5 percent, free beverages, 65+ (*).
    - Other Discounts: "Exclusive offers" available by e-mail or social media with signup.
7. **Dunkin' Donuts** www.dunkindonuts.com/dunkindonuts/en/promotions.html
    - Freebies: Free coffee on National Coffee Day (September 29) and Fridays has been known to happen.
    - Senior Discounts: AARP members get a free donut with a beverage purchase. Seniors 55 and over get 10 percent off or free coffee (*).
    - Other Discounts: 10 percent off on any order when you join the dunkindonuts.com e-mail list (*).
8. **Pizza Hut** www.pizzahut.com
    - Freebies: Free order of cheese sticks when you sign up for the "Hut Lovers" program.
    - Senior Discounts: 10 percent every Wednesday 60+ (*).
    - Other Discounts: Various carryout deals—$11 for any pizza ordered online, $10 dinner boxes.

9. **KFC** www.kfc.com/menu/promotions
    - Freebies: None found.
    - Senior Discounts: Free small drink with any meal for 55+ (*).
    - Other Discounts: Colonel's Club—a "venerated order" for special e-mail offers.
10. **Applebee's Neighborhood Grill & Bar** www.applebees.com
    - Freebies: Free birthday treat with Applebee's E-Club signup (*).
    - Senior Discounts: 10 to 15 percent off, varies by location, for 60+ with Golden Apple Card.
    - Other Discounts: $5 off first online or app order more than $25.
11. **Chick-fil-A** www.chick-fil-a.com
    - Freebies: One free entrée to anyone wearing anything cow-like on Cow Appreciation Day (July 12); free breakfast item for downloading app.
    - Senior Discounts: 10 percent discount or a free drink for 50 and over (*).
    - Other Discounts: Some through Chick-Fil-A E-mail Insiders club; large number through outside portals.
12. **Sonic Drive-In** www.sonicdrivein.com
    - Freebies: Free medium slush when you download the Sonic app and create an account.
    - Senior Discounts: 10 percent or free beverage for 60+ (varies by location).
    - Other Discounts: Monthly offers on main page (e.g., BOGO wings Monday through Thursday and 50 cent corn dogs).
13. **Olive Garden** www.olivegarden.com/specials
    - Freebies: Never Ending Pasta Bowl (free refills).
    - Senior Discounts: None found.

- Other Discounts: Deals on specials page; abundant on external portals.

14. **Chili's Grill & Bar** www.chilis.com
    - Freebies: Free menu item plus free dessert on your birthday for signing up for rewards program.
    - Senior Discounts: Offers vary by location.
    - Other Discounts: Rewards program; military, uniformed officer discounts also determined by location.
15. **Domino's Pizza** www.dominos.com
    - Freebies: "Piece of the Pie" rewards program: one free pizza for six online orders of $10 or more.
    - Senior Discounts: Occasional "50 percent off for seniors" deals lasting for a week, no age specified (*).
    - Other Discounts: National and local coupon assortment on coupons tab.
16. **Panera Bread** www.panera.com
    - Freebies: occasional free coffee and free bagel every day for a month campaigns.
    - Senior Discounts: Not an official policy but many franchised locations offer 10 percent (*).
    - Other discounts: 10 percent military and uniformed officer discount (*); others through rewards program.
17. **Jack in the Box** www.jackinthebox.com/offers
    - Freebies: Occasional free burger offers; Fan Club members get free dessert on birthday.
    - Senior Discounts: Up to 20 percent off for 55+.
    - Other Discounts: Offers by e-mail or mobile.
18. **Arby's** www.arbys.com/get-deals
    - Freebies: Free classic roast beef and drink when you sign up for deals by e-mail.
    - Senior Discounts: 10 percent or free small drink for 55+; varies by location (*).

- Other Discounts: E-mail coupons and deals ("Get Deals" page to sign up).

19. **Dairy Queen** www.dairyqueen.com/us-en/Promotions-US
    - Freebies: Join Blizzard Fan Club and get six BOGO Blizzard treat coupons.
    - Senior Discounts: 10 percent off, varies by location, no age given (*).
    - Other Discounts: Promotions U.S. page.
20. **Red Lobster** www.redlobster.com/specials
    - Freebies: Sign up for Free Catch Club and get a free appetizer or dessert and a surprise birthday offer.
    - Senior Discounts: None found.
    - Other Discounts: Through Fresh Catch Club.

CHAPTER 13

Getting In

Freebies and Discounts for Popular Admissions and Tickets

You want to spend a day doing something special, something out of the ordinary, something that takes you away from day-to-day life, and often away from home. You want to take the family to a museum, to a theme park, to a national park, to a state or local park, to a performing arts event, to spectator sport event, or to something you have to buy a ticket or an admission for.

Are there freebies and discounts available? Heck yes! Unless it's a wildly popular Paul McCartney concert or some such, marketers in these "businesses" are vying for your discretionary dollar just like everybody else. There are plenty of general discounts and benefits for these "ticketed" forms of entertainment and culture and a number of benefits for targeted groups like seniors and students. Freebies are harder to find, but they're out there—especially if you plan ahead and can be a bit flexible.

Museums

Naturally, most museums are local entities, not national chains, so I can't begin to capture them all here. But I'll give some guiding examples of what's available—and like always, a simple search will get you to the specific museum of choice.

Free Stuff and Services

You may never have to pay to get into a quality museum again! Most localities—I speak of cities for the most part—have "free museum days" where residents (and sometimes you have to prove this) can get into any of several museums in the area. Typically these days are known well in advance and are publicized and can be found on the Internet. A simple search for "museums free [city name]" will turn these freebies up, including info on museums that are free all the time. Some examples:

- *Smithsonian Museums*. Admission is free to all museums all the time. This may be the world's best museum freebie!
- *New York City*. NYC-Arts (www.nyc-arts.org) provides a list of museums that are free or free on certain days (or pay as you wish). See www.nyc-arts.org/collections/35/free-museum-days-or-pay-what-you-wish for this handy list of more than fifty museums.
- *Chicago*. ChooseChicago (www.choosechicago.com) publishes a list of free museum days by museum, with an alert to prove Illinois residency. For an article covering 2016, visit www.choosechicago.com/articles/view/free-museum-days-in-chicago/556/; 2017 was not yet available for this publication.
- *Los Angeles*. FreeMuseumDay.org provides a list of free museum days and "free always" museums in the LA area; there are 26 high-quality museums on the list.

- *Southern California*. The last Saturday in January is "Museums Free-for-All Day" for twenty museums in the area (see www.socalmuseums.org/free-for-all/).
- *Sacramento, California*. the first Saturday in February is "Museum Day"; 26 local museums provide free or half-off admissions (see sacmuseums.org/news-events/museum-day/).

Senior Discounts

Senior discounts are available at many but not all museums; typically these run in the 25 to 50 percent range. You may have to ask at the door. Most must be researched on a museum-by-museum basis, but there are some city-specific portals and websites to help out. Curiously I found that senior admission prices were more routinely available in some cities than others (New York, San Francisco, yes; Chicago, not so much).

Many price breaks are referred to as "senior admissions" prices rather than a discount, so a search for "museums senior discount [city name]" or "museum senior admission [city name]" will dig up gold:

- *New York City*. NYTix has a listing of ticket prices, including "Senior Citizen" prices, on their "Museums" page (www.nytix.com/Museums). The listing does not define age criteria.
- *San Francisco*. DeYoung museum (art) is $10 instead of $15; the SFMOMA (museum of modern art) is $22, not $25; both for 65 and over.
- *Denver* seniors can get into to the Denver Museum of Nature and Science for $11.95 instead of $14.95 and get $1 off at the IMAX Theater.

Other Deals and Discounts

This is a wide open field, with a number of evergreen and temporal discounts being available on deal portals. There are also important customer categories of discounts including student, teacher, military and so forth. These can be found through targeted searches—or just by asking:

- *Student discounts.* Most museums have a student discount; these typically mimic the senior discounts. The museum admission price listing at NYTix mentioned above (www.nytix.com/Museums) will give student prices in addition to prices for other categories.
- *Teacher discounts.* Many museums also recognize the value of their offerings to the education process and that teachers can evangelize the museum to a potent audience at a young age. The Perot Museum of Nature and Science lets K–12 teachers in for free. The Art Institute of Chicago gives free admission to Illinois K–12 teachers, teaching artists working in schools, and registered homeschool parents.
- *Military discounts.* Discounts here are less common, but the Field Museum in Chicago has free admission for active duty military personnel. Military discounts and free admissions are especially common for aviation, military, and similar museums.
- *Resident discounts.* Some museums in more tourist-driven locations give discounts to local residents: Chicago residents get $5 off on a Field Museum admission.
- *Deal portals.* If the deals cited above aren't enough, deal and coupon portals like Groupon often carry several city-specific deals, typically for peripheral museums you may not have heard about (hence the deal!). Want to check

out the Museum of the American Gangster in New York City? A Groupon deal gets half off on a visit for two, a $20 savings—no guns or shooting required!

Theme and Amusement Parks

Okay, so maybe museums bore you a little—you'd rather take yourself and the family for a day of thrills on the biggest roller coaster around! Here are some freebies, deals, and discounts within the theme park theme.

Free Stuff and Services

Other than sneaking in (there's actually a YouTube video on this!) or getting free parking to go with an otherwise-expensive admission, there isn't much free in the world of theme and amusement parks. The few freebies include the following:

- *Coney Island, Brooklyn, New York.* Admission to the seaside parks, boardwalk, and beach is still free.
- Some parks still offer free admission and make their take the old fashioned way on ride ticket and refreshment sales. Check out the time-tested family owned Knoebels Amusement Resort in Elysburg, Pennsylvania (near but not that near to Harrisburg, Pennsylvania), or Family Kingdom in Myrtle Beach, South Carolina. Yeah, these are not completely free, but it's a step in the right direction, especially for those families weary of the hundreds spent just to get into a Disney theme park.
- *Free admission for military personnel and dependents.* There are a few parks that offer such freebies, and they're worthwhile—including Sea World and Busch Gardens parks, among others. See the Military.com portal noted below.

Senior Discounts

Outright senior discounts are not easy to find in the theme park world—guessing seniors aren't a major target group in this industry. A recent search on AARP came up empty, although there were a few discounts available on Expedia.com for AARP members. See the Expedia-branded AARP Travel Center (www.expedia-aarp.com).

Other Deals and Discounts

Discounts for major theme and amusement parks are not that hard to find if you look around. Many are offered through local visitors bureaus (see www.visitororlando.com for deals in Orlando, Florida, for example) or through coupon portals.

- *Military discounts* are plentiful enough so that amusement parks have their own page on the Military.com portal (www.military.com/discounts/amusement-parks).
- *Theme park ticket portals.* There are a few, including Discount Tickets and Tours (www.discountticketsandtours.com), that offer decent deals.
- *Costco.* The giant warehouse retailer has gotten into selling packaged tickets, usually multiple ticket or multiple day passes, at worthwhile discounts if you plan ahead. See www.costco.com/theme-parks.html.
- *Groupon* and others offer deals tailored to your locale for local amusements, such as Sky High Sports (trampoline play) and others, and for national attractions if you search for the destination city. The parks aren't always the top billings in the area, but the discounts are significant.

National, State, and Local Parks

Some people like the action, thrill, or showmanship of an amusement or theme park; others like the natural beauty, peace and quiet, recreation, and sometimes the history found in a national, state, or local park. As government budgets have become more constrained over the years, parks have had to raise their admission fees, and some have, frankly, become cash cows to support other parks in the system—Yosemite National Park in California now charges $30 for a single car admission.

The freebies and discounts in this category won't make you rich, but every bit helps. There are, of course, thousands of state and local parks, so this is far from an all-inclusive guide.

Free Stuff and Services

Parks are for the people, and many park systems, recognizing that and recognizing the burden of park admission fees on the average family, have free admission days.

- *Free-admission days in national parks.* In 2016, the National Park Service designated sixteen "free admission" days, including the entire weekend of August 25 through 28 for the one hundredth birthday of the National Park System. The dates can be found at the National Parks website (www.nps.gov/planyourvisit/fee-free-parks-state.htm) or the National Park Foundation website (www.nationalparks.org). Watch out, however—some parks can become very crowded on these days.
- Many state parks systems, such as national parks, offer free admission days—search for "[state] state parks free" or similar. Some parks offer free camping on certain days or in certain seasons. Colorado offers free admission

to all state parks on Colorado Day, August 1, the anniversary of the state's 1876 entry into the Union. A similar search can be done for county, city, and other local parks.

Senior Discounts

Now we come to the standard bearer of all senior discounts:

- *National Park Senior Passes, once known as Golden Age Passports.* Instead of paying $80 per year for an annual pass or $10 here and $20 there for individual admissions, if you're 62 and over, you can buy a Senior Pass, which gets you into national parks and more than two thousand other federal lands and facilities, for $10 *for life.* That's right—*$10, one time, for life.* The pass is not only good for national parks but also national monuments, historic sites, recreation areas, and wildlife refuges.
- *State and local senior discounts.* Many state and local park systems have gotten into the senior discount game, though few are as generous as the federal government. The State of California offers $1 off for day use and $2 for camping for 62 and over. Nevada seniors 65+ can buy an annual state parks pass for $30 instead of $65 to $85; Vermonters 62+ can get free day use for life. Many discounts are available for camping or other recreational activities. Check the website for the park or park system in question.

Other Deals and Discounts

Deals and discounts show up in many of the usual categories—military and disabled especially. I did not find many student or teacher discounts. Seasonal discounts are abundant, particularly for lodging in the park in question. Many states like

Ohio and Tennessee allow you to sign up for an e-mail newsletter featuring deals primarily on lodging and camping.

- *Military discounts.* The National Park Service offers even a better deal than the Senior Pass to active military—free admission, including dependents. Well, better if you don't take into account the fact that the Senior Pass is for life.
- *Disability.* The National Park Service offers a free-for-lifetime access pass to those with a permanent disability with proper paperwork done in advance. Many states, such as Texas, with a 50 percent discount, follow suit.
- *Winter discounts.* Kentucky state parks and many others offer discounted admissions and lodging in the winter; 50 percent discounts are not uncommon.

Music, Theater, and Performing Arts

Music, theater, and performing arts is an extremely broad category with multiple offerings in every locale. As with—and maybe more than with—other categories, you're best off relying on search engines to find the deal you want for the event or artist you want to see.

Free Stuff and Services

For the most part, "free" is a matter of finding a free venue, which isn't hard to do with the right search: "[type of performance or artist] [city or locale] free" will get some results. Among the more consistent bets for free performances are the following:

- *Local advertiser–sponsored free events.* Often these come in the form of outdoor concerts sponsored by a local bank or some such or a consortium of local sponsors. They're usually well publicized but are also normally on the web and available by search. Bring your folding chairs and a blanket and enjoy! Some indoor theater and concert events follow this path too.

- *Local school performing arts.* Local schools and especially colleges, universities, and performing arts colleges can provide a number of high-quality performing arts shows, concerts, and recitals for free or for modest fees. If you live near such a learning institution, find your way to their music school page or similar and get familiar with their schedule—it's usually the best deal out there. The Music, Theatre, Dance, Film, and Visual Arts page at Brigham Young University (arts.byu.edu) is but one good example.

Senior Discounts

Like museums covered earlier, senior "discounts" are abundant and tend to be offered in the form of special senior pricing, often as much as 50 percent off normal ticket prices, to lure seniors out of their comfortable living rooms. A few examples:

- *Ford's Theater*, Washington, D.C., offers 50 percent senior (and student) discounts for age 65+ on the day of the performance. Other D.C. area venues, such as the John F. Kennedy Center for the Performing Arts, offer similar discounts.
- *The Music Center* (Los Angeles) offers limited numbers of $20 "Student and Senior Rush" tickets for each performance to be purchased up to ninety minutes before the performance. Regular tickets can be many times that amount. Be agile and willing to stand in line. (See www.musiccenter.org.)

- *The Denver Center for the Performing Arts* offers a combination of the above two: 50 percent off for seniors 62+ ("Senior Rush") an hour before the performance.

Other Deals and Discounts

Many performing arts organizations offer the standard set of "category" discounts for military, students, teachers, and the disabled. Some also sell deeply discounted tickets within short time periods before the show to fill venues, squeeze out a few extra bucks, and get people to attend who might not otherwise do so.

- *Discounted Broadway tickets, New York.* For years, Broadway's own Theater Development Fund has received and sold donated, unsold Broadway theater tickets at their iconic "TKTS" booth on Times Square and other NYC locations, usually the afternoon of the day of the show. The proceeds go to support actors and various theater programs; buyers usually get 50 percent off on Broadway and off-Broadway shows where surplus tickets are available. (Want to see *The Book of Mormon* or another off-the-charts popular show? Fuggetaboudit.) While TKTS booths still operate as sentimental favorites, you can do this online now too at an assortment of sites (search "discount Broadway tickets"). If you're not planning to travel to NYC, this day-of-the-show discount model is popular elsewhere.
- *The Denver Center for the Performing Arts* (I'll use this example again) offers 20 percent off on all tickets and 50 percent off on tickets purchased an hour before the show like for seniors described above and for active and retired military personnel and their immediate families. Student "Rush" tickets can be had for $10 up to an hour

before as available. Many, maybe most, arts entities offer similar discounts.

- *"EBT" card or similar.* If you're in an income bracket low enough to receive food stamps, you may be eligible for deeply discounted tickets. If you have such an "Electronic Benefits Transfer" card in Oregon, you can get into any of Portland's five major centers for the arts for $5. This sort of cultural outreach benefits the recipients in many ways, helps fill up venues, and strengthens the community—a classic civic win-win-win.

Spectator Sports

For many, the best and most sought-after diversion may be a well-contested sports game. But as you may have experienced, especially if professional sports is involved, the cost—and especially the total cost—of attending almost any kind of game can be daunting, especially if you're taking the family along. Once again, if you're willing to be a little flexible, there are deals to be had.

Free Stuff and Services

Not too surprisingly, most sports at the professional level are played with the intent to pay the players and to compensate the team(s) for their expenses, so you have to look a bit "outside the box" to find the freebies. There are two main avenues to watch sports for free—if you're willing to give up the "professional level."

- *College sports.* If you live near a college and especially a university, you may not get into the Saturday afternoon football game for free, but unless it's Ohio State or some other top team, it will be cheaper than the pro counterpart.

What is free are the many sports off that top-tier grid. Baseball, track and field, soccer, gymnastics, even hockey, and others are often free to attend. The University of Illinois at Champaign-Urbana publishes a list of free sports at tickets.fightingillini.com; searches for schools near you may well yield similar info.

- *High school and other sports.* If you're willing to go one rung down the food chain, there are a lot more free sports events to attend. Local high school and community colleges field a lot of dreams in a lot of sports. These events are usually not that well attended, so not only are they free but you can sit practically right on the field or court. In a given area, the vast choice of schools expands the possibilities.

Senior Discounts

Senior discounts are available for some events and not for others. Ticketmaster.com puts it simply: "To see if the event you are purchasing tickets for has any senior citizen discounts, please search for the event from our homepage and check the available ticket types." (See help.ticketmaster.com/senior-citizen-discounts/.)

Other Deals and Discounts

- *Practice sessions.* If you're flexible with time and sometimes with distance, you can watch professional caliber sports for a modest price (and there are probably some "free" chances to observe, I just didn't dig that deep). A Golden State Warriors practice session recently offered tickets in the home arena for a preseason practice for a mere $5, a tiny fraction of the regular price. You can probably "sit down low" as well.

- *Military, student, and other "category" discounts.* Depending on the sport, the venue, and other factors, at least these two category factors may be in play. If you think you may be eligible for one of these discounts, look at the ticket listing, search the site for "military discount" or "student discount" and be prepared to ask the ticket seller in person about these discounts if you're buying in person.

Deals and discounts in the spectator sports category are a bit tough to find, especially at the top levels. Just remember—screaming and shouting and carrying on at the event once in and at your seat is completely free!

CHAPTER 14
Doing It

Freebies and Discounts for Popular Recreation and Pastimes

Recreation comes in all sizes and shapes, and our society has a lot more time to enjoy the many and increasing forms of it. I can't begin to cover all the opportunities to get outdoors, to have fun, and to experience leisure every way from quietly reading a book to yelling and screaming your way down a gnarly white-water rafting course.

What I can do is pretty much what I've done throughout the book—grab a few good examples of the kinds of freebies, deals, and discounts you'll find in this space, then turn you loose to dig up your own! So here goes . . .

Movies

We Americans are a nation of moviegoers. However, consumer electronics technology and the advent of content in the home from Netflix and the like have made us a nation of movie-at-homers as well. I'll give a short overview of ways to avoid paying full price for the many movies you're likely to take in these days.

Free Stuff and Services

Believe it or not, even though they get nine bucks a bucket for popcorn these days, there are some ways to watch movies for free. And with popcorn that expensive, there are plenty of reasons besides the cost of the movie to find alternatives:

- *At the theater—for free.* It doesn't happen all the time, and it doesn't happen everywhere. But there are individual and chain theaters, sometimes a whole community of theaters together, that offer free movies from time to time as a community service and gesture of goodwill to local moviegoers. In Phoenix, Arizona, for example, a number of theaters work together providing free movies—good ones—for children home for the summer in daytime on Tuesdays, Wednesdays, and Thursdays (what else are kids supposed to do when it's 117 degrees outside?). A search for "free movies theater [your community]" should get you a seat.

  Some communities provide free outdoor movies in the summer, again as a community service event for the local populace. New York City has dozens of them every summer—see www.thrillist.com/events/new-york/all-the-free-outdoor-movies-in-nyc-summer-2016 as an example of one of many guides. Search for "free movies outdoor [your community]," and you're likely to find a movie under the stars—but you'll have to bring your own popcorn.
- *At the library.* Libraries were once pretty constrained to stock movies with educational or historic value—classics and documentaries on polar bears and such. Not so much anymore. Libraries stock thousands of movies and while you won't find too many explicit movies, there's a pretty

decent selection these days of more popular titles like perhaps *Saving Private Ryan* or *The Bourne Identity*.

- *Free movie portals*. For those who prefer their free movies to arrive over the Internet (and who have a fast enough "pipe" to bring them in), there are free on-demand movie streaming services. A few names (and this is an easy search) include Crackle (www.crackle.com), 123Movies (123movies.to), and xmovies8.tv. These sites, like Netflix (which isn't free but feels like it after you pay the small monthly charge), may not have the latest or best-quality pictures—but hey, they're free. For a slightly more cultured assortment with a lot of "indie," classic, and foreign films, check out OpenCulture (www.openculture.com). These free services are usually paid for with advertising and a fairly explicit promise to collect data to learn your viewing habits and interests for the Big Data world.

Senior Discounts

Seniors are an important target market for movie theaters, especially since they normally can fill empty seats on weekdays. Discounts are easy to find, although some are more structured and transparent than others:

- *AMC Theaters* gives a 30 percent discount to seniors (60+), with most locations giving a 60 percent discount on Tuesdays.
- *Showcase Cinemas* has "Senior Wednesdays" where seniors 60+ can get a discounted admission of $6.50 plus a popcorn and soda for $3.50 (now *there's* the real savings!)
- *Regal Cinemas* have special senior pricing which varies by movie and time for seniors 60 and over.

- *United Artists* offers $8 tickets printed in advance for AARP members (and a $3 discount on popcorn).
- Most other theater chains have some form of discount or senior pricing. Search "[name of theater chain] senior discount." If you don't get much, try "senior pricing"—many just quote a senior price something less than full adult price.

Other Deals and Discounts

Promotions and offers are fairly abundant in this arena, but for the most part, you won't save very much money unless you're an avid moviegoer, and you probably won't save on the hottest movies on a Saturday night. Again, some of these "deals" are more transparent than others:

- *Military discounts.* Most theater chains offer reduced military pricing (not discounts). The pricing can vary by movie and time and be a bit difficult to discern until you go to buy your tickets.
- *Student discounts.* A few but not all chains offer student pricing or discounts. Some are transparent and consistent from one day and one movie to the next. Marcus Theaters offers $5 pricing for any movie on Thursdays and a free popcorn with a valid student ID.
- *Bargain Tuesdays (and other days).* Tuesday is the most common—United Artists gives 50 percent off and Showcase offers regular admission for $8 on Tuesdays for everyone.
- *Coupon portals.* Groupon offers a "Fandango" page with free and discounted movie ticket coupons; the discounts were rather small when I researched it—$2 off on three or more tickets.

- *Costco and other warehouse clubs.* If you go to a lot of movies, Costco offers ten-packs for AMC and Regal Cinemas for $89.99, Cinemark for $84.99, and others—saving $10 to $20 across ten admissions. There are also four-packs for $35.99 ($33.99 for Cinemark)—only a slightly smaller savings.

Books, Newspapers, and Magazines

As both a pleasure and a pastime and as a source of learning, few categories can compete with books and their newspaper and magazine brethren. If you read a lot, you know that the cost of these media, especially books, can add up quickly!

Free Stuff and Services

Of course, since the founding of our country, public libraries have been the outstanding resource for books, newspapers, and other periodicals. But the advent of e-books (which takes a lot of the cost out of manufacturing a book) has brought "free" into the book vocabulary in new ways.

- *Libraries.* They're worth mentioning again because not only do they provide thousands of free books and a sanctuary in which to read them but they also offer an extraordinary assortment of other media that we tend to overlook, especially if we haven't been to one in a while. The magazine and newspaper shelves are well stocked. These days, most libraries have added collections of audiobooks, films and TV shows (on DVD) to extend their offering to other platforms. Many also lend out e-books, so you don't even have to go to the library itself if you don't want to. Most of us have gotten out of the habit—but libraries aren't what they used to be; they've come a long way.

- *Free e-books.* The advent of e-books has made it so much easier for writers to write and produce a book that many do without regard to financial gain, thus there are a lot of free books out there. Likewise, there are classics where copyrights have expired (seventy-five years for most). Both types of books are made available for free in a number of places. Apple carries a lot of free books in its iBooks store. FreePopularBooks (www.freepopularbooks.com) and BookBub (www.bookbub.com) are free book portals—but they do require an e-mail address and/or an app download before you check out what's free (a million titles, as they advertise). Easier to use and with "only" 53,000 "high-quality" books is Project Gutenberg (www.gutenberg.org), which operates on user donations.
- *Free magazines.* There are a few sites that purvey free copies of major magazines as PDF files or through an app on your mobile device. I haven't tried these, but you could look at Read Magazines (www.read-magazines.com) or Magzus (www.magzus.com).

Senior Discounts

Type in "books senior discount" in a search engine, and you get books (like this one) explaining how to get senior discounts. Not exactly what I had in mind. Type in "senior discount on books" and you get pretty much the same result—nothing. "Bookseller senior discount"? You get job ads for senior booksellers at certain book stores. Finally, feeling a little frustrated, I searched for "Barnes and Noble senior discount." I got a teen book listing for a collection of syndicated "For Better or For Worse" comics called *Senior's Discount: A For Better or For Worse Collection*. Below that was a listing for an AARP discount page. Ah! I exclaimed hopefully. But when I arrived there were sixteen books on the page, all published by AARP, with titles like *5 Secrets to Brain Health*.

I give up. There will be no senior discounts on books or other related media noted in this book. That doesn't mean there aren't a few out there. Somewhere.

Other Deals and Discounts

Books are expensive. As are magazines and newspapers. As a consequence, sellers and publishers run frequent promotions, and especially if you buy books frequently, some of them are worth the time—and sometimes the money—invested.

- *Barnes & Noble.* While they sell most books at full retail cover price, you can get some savings if you work at it. You can sign up for the B&N Membership for $25 and you get 10 percent off on everything in the store (including gifts, gift cards, even Starbucks coffee) and other coupon offers. Get on their mailing list, and you'll get regular 20 to 40 percent off coupons. Their "buy two get one free" specials, usually on popular trade paperbacks, are good deals too. I should note that many smaller booksellers have similar programs.
- *Business and corporate discounts.* Many booksellers give special discounts to business customers, especially if you're in the media or book business yourself (the assumption is you'll buy a lot of research material and send customers to the store to buy your product). These discounts can be as high as 20 percent, and they usually take a pretty broad perspective on who qualifies—if you want the discount you're probably going to buy a lot. Talk to a manager at your favorite bookstore, especially if it is a large one or a chain. At Barnes & Noble, they push you toward the B&N

Membership program, which comes with a $25 annual fee. The membership allows you a 40 percent discount on most hardcover books and a 10 percent discount on other purchases.

- *Educator and student discounts.* Barnes & Noble has an educator discount card program, saving 20 percent, but no direct student discount. With other book outlets, it's worth asking. There are no current educator or student discounts at Amazon—if you ask, you are directed to Amazon Prime.
- *Coupon and deal portals.* Most of the major deal portals have an assortment of book and book-related coupons, some for specific books, some just for general discounts and promotions at stores. RetailMeNot (www.retailmenot.com) has a particularly large coupon repository from multiple booksellers and other stores at www.retailmenot.com/coupons/books.

Hobbies, Arts, and Crafts

Many of us with a creative stripe or simply with plenty of time on our hands choose to create or collect things. As anybody who does this actively knows, it can get pretty "spendy" over time. Compared to some categories, the number of arts and crafts supplies sellers is rather limited, but the nature of this pastime makes it well worth their efforts to gain and keep your loyalty. So there are plenty of freebies and deals out there.

Free Stuff and Services

In a manner similar to auto parts stores, hobby, art, and craft stores offer an assortment of free "how-to" materials to get you started and keep you going; there are other freebie "how-to" resources as well.

- *Hobby Lobby.* This large retailer's "DIY Projects and Videos" page (www.hobbylobby.com/c/13) offers project ideas, plans, and videos for fifteen categories of projects. "Live a Creative Life" is the apt slogan. They also offer classes at their stores, some free, some at a modest cost.
- *Michaels.* Another large retailer with a wide assortment of classes, some online. (See www.michaels.com/classes-and-events/classesandevents.)
- *Pinterest.* This shared content "catalog of ideas" site also offers a well-stocked and free "DIY and crafts" page.
- Free content portal Gizmo's publishes a summary of "Arts and Crafts and Hobbies eBooks and Written Instructions" (42 entries at last count); see www.techsupportalert.com/free-books-arts-crafts-hobbies.

Senior Discounts

Hobbyists are (1) creative and (2) have time, and guess who typically has the time and the grandchildren to make things for? Okay, this is stereotypical, but seniors are a recognized group in this category. That said, retailing giant Hobby Lobby appears to prefer the "let's make a deal for everyone" approach.

- *Michaels* offers 10 percent off most items to seniors 55+ every day—some exclusions apply.
- *JoAnn Stores* has senior discount days, most recently 20 percent off for 55+. (See www.joann.com/seniordiscountday/.)

Other Deals and Discounts

Most of the major deal and discount portals have hobby and craft discounts and deals, and the major retailers carry plenty of coupons and deals on their sites as well. Notables include the following:

- *Goodshop*. This deal portal has a well-defined "Art, Crafts & Hobbies" page under its "Home" category (www.goodsearch.com/art-crafts-hobbies-category/coupons) with plenty of deals for large and small retailers, including scrapbook and quilting suppliers and other niche players.
- *GoodSavers*. Another deal portal I haven't mentioned much but that has a well-stocked "Crafts & Hobbies" page, again with a lot of small "niche-y" suppliers, accessible directly from the homepage (www.goodsavers.com).
- *Michaels*. Significant daily and two-day deals right on their homepage (www.michaels.com)
- *Hobby Lobby*. They do their deals on a "Weekly Ad" page (www.hobbylobby.com/find-savings) and offers a 40 percent off one item at regular price deal at all times.
- *Specific search*. You can search for the hobby or craft itself—"[hobby] deals and discounts." My search for "scrapbooking deals and discounts" led me right to the coupon page for Scrapbook.com (www.scrapbook.com/coupons). It's easier than spray-painting pine cones!

Bowling, Golf, Skiing, and Watersports

Finally, when a lot of us think of "leisure" we think of "recreation" and the personal/social sports of bowling, golf, skiing, watersports, and many others. Here again there are many sellers competing for your precious discretionary dollars. While the purveyors in this space are primarily local—not national chains—there are a lot of deals to be had!

Free Stuff and Services

Free stuff in this category usually comes in the form of loyalty program benefits and free instruction for simpler activities like surfing or paddle boarding. Free transportation services, such as offered by some ski resorts, are also available. As usual, a search for "[activity] [location] free" will return some of the usually pretty short list of free offers. A few examples:

- *Kids Bowl Free.* Normally I don't get too excited about free deals for kids with paying parents. But this is a good idea—register your kids and they get two free games *every day* all summer long at selected bowling centers across the country (www.kidsbowlfree.com).
- *Free "golf games."* I couldn't find any free golf offers, and I'm not much of a video game junkie and thus consider a "free" game to not have enough value to mention (and so I don't throughout this book). But if you search for "free golf," a smorgasbord of free golf games and simulators come up, who knows, some of them might actually help your game. Look at www.freewebarcade.com/golf-games.php, but make sure you do the real thing once in a while at least when the weather's good!
- *Free BOGO ski lift ticket with Shell gas purchase.* The best seasonal skiing freebie I've found and ordinarily I wouldn't consider it "free" because you have to buy gas. But most of us have to buy gas anyway, so to get a free lift ticket, which can be worth more than $100 in some places is a pretty good deal. I've been surprised how good this deal is, how many resorts it's good for, and how long it's lasted. (See www.skifreedeals.com/; info can also be found in Shell stations in or adjacent to popular ski resort areas.)

- *Free online boating courses.* The BoatUS Foundation offers free online boating safety courses tailored to each state. (See www.boatus.org/courses.)
- *Free kayaking in New York City.* Stuck in Manhattan or Brooklyn on a sweltering summer afternoon? The Brooklyn Bridge Boathouse (www.bbpboathouse.org) and the NYC Downtown Boathouse (www.downtownboathouse.org) offer free kayaking for twenty minutes (longer if others aren't waiting).
- *Island Water Sports* of Deerfield Beach, Florida, offers free surf, stand up paddle boarding, and skimboarding lessons every Saturday from 7 to 9 a.m. (See www.islandcamps.com/free-lessons/.)

Senior Discounts

For many recreational activities, seniors are an important market. A lot of them participate, and they tend to do it at off peak times; they may also bring their families. Discounts are widely available but can be a little hard to find; your best bet is to check out the website of the particular purveyor or facility—or just ask. Often the right term is "senior rate" or "senior green fee"—not a senior "discount" per se.

- Senior discounts are available at many bowling alleys but tend to be modest—maybe a buck off on a $9 game. Red Rock Lanes of Las Vegas, Nevada, offers $1.50 games Sunday through Thursday after 10 p.m. for senior night owls.
- *Golf senior discounts* and senior rates are widely available and may save 20 to 30 percent on normal greens fees. Some courses or municipalities sell a "senior card" which may entitle you to even deeper discounts. The best approach here (no pun intended) is to check the website of the course in question.

- Senior discounts are abundant at ski resorts; the resorts probably feel if there are older folks around, everyone else will be tempted to ski for life; most also don't ski the whole day. Discounts of 33 to 50 percent are common, mostly for 65 and over. See www.liftopia.com, find your favorite resort, and search for senior tickets.
- *AARP discounts.* AARP members can get 15 percent off "deal" tee times booked on TeeOff (www.teeoff.com).

Other Deals and Discounts

Freebies are limited, and senior discounts are common but not a main part of the marketing effort for most recreation providers. Where the rubber meets the road is in other deals and discounts—deals are very abundant and typically highly temporal—they depend on the season and just how busy the provider is at the moment.

- *Groupon.* This large deal portal works best for the recreation category, as it is well organized and points directly to deals in your area. The thread runs through "Things to Do," and of course you can search for any activity. "Fun and Leisure" is a popular category. Deals for bowling, golf, and watersports were running 40 to 50 percent off; I didn't see anything for skiing, for it was out of season. Other coupon portals are good but tended to focus more on equipment, less on the activity.
- Military and student discounts are fairly abundant at most recreational operators, but you may have to ask.
- *Skiing.* Buy online and in advance. Portal Liftopia (www.liftopia.com) offers most tickets at a discount, as much as 33 percent, though still pretty expensive!
- *Golf.* Similar to Liftopia for skiing, TeeOff.com (www.teeoff.com) offers discounts to folks who can plan their

rounds in advance. What's nice about TeeOff and other tee-time booking apps is that you can search among all the days' available times and the course can offer different pricing for those times; you can find the best deal that fits your schedule (and heat tolerance, etc.).

CHAPTER 15

Buying It

Retail and Merchandising Freebies and Discounts

Finally, when it comes to deals, most of us think of retailers before we think of anything else—although the deal and coupon portals are gaining ground fast in this regard. I will close this book by providing a summary of freebie, deal, and discount offerings and where to find them for the top thirty U.S. retailers by sales. The list is amended somewhat to remove some of the more localized grocery chains and is presented in alphabetical order.

By nature, true freebies are hard to find, although some come as "BOGO" offers, some as free shipping on occasion from their online operations, and some from loyalty programs. If you do a search for "[retailer] free," you often come up with "free store pickup," meaning you can buy something online and pick it up at the store for free—without delivery charges. That's a no-brainer, and I won't even elaborate on these offers in what follows as freebies. I also won't elaborate on "BOGO" offers in great detail; these are really discounts when you think about it.

Discounts are largely temporal, mimic each other, and can be found in abundance both on their websites and on deal portals.

Generally the deal portal "deals" are similar or the same as those found on the retailer site, but for some retailers, that isn't the case. For retail deals, I'll steer you toward RetailMeNot (www.retailmenot.com), which organizes its deals by retailer and caters to the retail industry, in contrast to Groupon and others, which tend to be more organized by item. I'll give a "deal count" I observed for the day I put this summary together as a barometer for the retailer's "deal" activity.

And for seniors? Senior discount days are worth watching out for—and vary considerably among retailers. It seems like some retailers—but not all—have moved away from special treatment for seniors in favor of making better deals for everyone. Like chain restaurants (Chapter 12) many of these deals are invisible in company websites and are found anecdotally by customers or journalists covering such things. Those situations are marked with an "(*)." Finally, some retailers offer military, veteran, student, and teacher/educator discounts; I've highlighted these where I've come across them.

Happy shopping!

Ace Hardware www.acehardware.com

- Free Stuff and Services: None noted.
- Senior Discounts: 10 percent discount, 60+ (though reported to be age 55 to 65, depending on location, as Ace is a loosely knit confederation of franchisees).
- Other Deals and Discounts: Weekly "ad" with specials (see "Sales & Specials" tab). Limited deals through deal portals—20 deals on RetailMeNot.

Amazon.com

- Free Stuff and Services: Their "Amazon Prime" service for $99 per year isn't free, but if you're a heavy user, it will seem free after a while. Free two-day shipping and

free music and other content are a part of this program, and they also offer free trials of this service. Worth a look.
- Senior Discounts: None noted.
- Other Deals and Discounts: Abundant specials on their website (see "Today's Deals" tab). Moderate deal portal activity—46 offers.

Apple Store www.apple.com/retail/
- Free Stuff and Services: Based on my own experience, their "Genius Bar" righted the ship on my old iPad for free, which I didn't expect (might vary by location, and the wait time cost was significant but worth it). Free apps, books, and other content through iTunes are also worth noting.
- Senior Discounts: None noted, but there is a free Senior Discounts app!
- Other Deals and Discounts: No "deals" page. The best deals noted are for students and educators at qualifying schools, who may receive as much as 15 percent off a Mac or 5 percent off an iPad (*; see www.apple.com/us-hed/shop). Moderate deal portal activity—30 offers.

AutoZone www.autozone.com
- Free Stuff and Services: They offer a host of free automotive diagnostic services (see www.autozone.com/inourstores/services.jsp).
- Senior Discounts: None noted.
- Other Deals and Discounts: Check "Deals" page (www.autozone.com/deals/). Not as much happening on deal portals—ten offers; top "offer" simply redirects you to their deals page. Veterans can receive a 10 percent discount (*).

Bed Bath & Beyond www.bedbathandbeyond.com

- Free Stuff and Services: Free shipping offers for online orders.
- Senior Discounts: None found.
- Other Deals and Discounts: Famous for their regular 20 percent off one item coupons mostly distributed by mail and also available on their website. But they plan to discontinue these in favor of a membership discount and free shipping service modeled after Amazon Prime. Main web page is full of offers, and you can sign up for more by e-mail. Veterans and families can receive a 10 percent discount (*). Moderate portal activity—43 offers.

Best Buy www.bestbuy.com

- Free Stuff and Services: Occasional free setup offers on tech products through their Geek Squad subsidiary, free two-day shipping offers.
- Senior Discounts: None noted.
- Other Deals and Discounts: Extensive on-site deals at deals.bestbuy.com—weekly ad, daily deals, outlet and open box, and deals for college students. Veterans can receive a 10 percent discount, varies by store (*). Moderate deal portal activity—29 offers.

BJ's Wholesale Club www.bjs.com

- Free Stuff and Services: Free "one-day" passes and free trial memberships through main website and deal portals. Free additional household members.
- Senior Discounts: None noted.
- Other Deals and Discounts: Deals and discounts on main page and more "push" deals when you buy "Inner Circle" membership for $50. Fairly extensive portal activity—49 deals including free trial memberships noted above.

Costco www.costco.com

- Free Stuff and Services: Free shipping offers from Costco.com. No free trials noted.
- Senior Discounts: None noted.
- Other Deals and Discounts: On main page or "View Warehouse Coupons" link. Little deal portal activity—only six offers.

CVS Caremark www.cvs.com

- Free Stuff and Services: None noted.
- Senior Discounts: None noted.
- Other Deals and Discounts: Weekly deals, e-mail offers, a 20 percent off shopping pass when you get a flu shot, and similar offers. Low deal portal activity—13 offers.

Dick's Sporting Goods www.dickssportinggoods.com

- Free Stuff and Services: Free shipping on orders $49 and over.
- Senior Discounts: None noted.
- Other Deals and Discounts: Military and veterans can receive a 10 percent discount. "Flash" sales on website, other deals on main page, $10 off when you spend $50, and buy online and pick up in store. Clearance items page. Moderate portal activity— at 34 offers.

Dollar General www.dollargeneral.com

- Free Stuff and Services: Occasional "free" coupons for small items.
- Senior Discounts: None noted.
- Other Deals and Discounts: Mostly done through coupons, see "Coupons" link on main page. Fairly low portal activity—21 offers.

Family Dollar Stores www.familydollar.com

- Free Stuff and Services: None noted.

- Senior Discounts: Select offers for AARP members.
- Other Deals and Discounts: Extensive deals on website; see "Weekly Ads" and "Smart Coupons" tabs. Very low portal activity—five offers.

Gap Stores www.gap.com

- Free Stuff and Services: Free shipping on $50 Gap.com purchase.
- Senior Discounts: Banana Republic (one of their brands) offers 10 percent off to 62+ (*). Could not find similar discounts in other Gap stores.
- Other Deals and Discounts: E-mail signup gets special offers and 25 percent off on certain regular items; other offers on main page. Extensive portal offers—73 offers for Gap-branded store alone.

Home Depot www.homedepot.com

- Free Stuff and Services: Regular free workshops and demos to learn how to do projects.
- Senior Discounts: None found.
- Other Deals and Discounts: Plenty of deals and discounts on main page, also on "Savings Center" page neatly organized by product category (see www.homedepot.com/c/Savings_Center). Active and retired military personnel get 10 percent discount. Low to moderate deal portal activity—21 deals.

JC Penney www.jcpenney.com

- Free Stuff and Services: It's not really "free" but JC Penney has "tax-free weekends" typically during the back-to-school shopping season. It should be thought of as a small discount, but it feels "free."
- Senior Discounts: None found.
- Other Deals and Discounts: Very active with deals and discounts on own site—on main page and on

"Coupons & Extra Savings" tab. Fairly active on deal portals—39 deals.

Kohl's www.kohls.com

- Free Stuff and Services: Free shipping on orders greater than $75.
- Senior Discounts: Senior discount days—15 percent every Wednesday. Best in class.
- Other Deals and Discounts: Military discount of 15 percent but can vary by store (*). Main page very busy with deals including a $10 off on $50 spent online week long deal, a "Today's Deals" section, "Bonus Buys"—you could spend a day searching through them all. Active on deal portals— with 45 active deals.

Kroger www.kroger.com

These can vary by subsidiary:

- Free Stuff and Services: "Free Friday Downloads" usually contain a few small freebies. Free M&Ms on National M&M's Day was a recent example.
- Senior Discounts: Senior Citizen Reward Club includes 5 percent to 10 percent discount first Wednesday of every month for 60 and over but reportedly being phased out. Fred Meyer subsidiary has a 10 percent discount on the first Tuesday of every month for those 55 and over. Fry's has a 10 percent discount on the first Wednesday every month (55+). Harris Teeter has a 5 percent discount every Thursday (60+) (*).
- Other Deals and Discounts: "Free Friday Downloads," "Weekly Ad and Coupons" tabs on main page, only three portal deals for Kroger itself and two for big-box-format Fred Meyer subsidiary—so not very active on portals.

Lowe's www.lowes.com

- Free Stuff and Services: Free shipping on orders of $49 or more.
- Senior Discounts: None found.
- Other Deals and Discounts: Military discount of 10 percent, including families (*). Veterans get 10 percent on Veteran's Day, Independence Day, and Memorial Day (*). There is a 5 percent discount for using a Lowe's credit card. Best deals are on main page, also a "Shop Savings and Weekly Ad" tab at the bottom of the page. Not very active on deal portals—seven deals.

Macy's www.macys.com

- Free Stuff and Services: Various free shipping offers.
- Senior Discounts: None found.
- Other Deals and Discounts: Many offers. Some are complex and require a return visit—for example, 20 percent off next purchase for buying online and picking up in store. Frequent discounts for using Macy's card. Very active with other deals and offers, see main page and also well-stocked "Deals & Promotions" tab—but be careful to read the fine print. Also active in the online portals—50 deals available—most for purchase from macys.com matching in store prices.

Nordstrom www.nordstom.com

- Free Stuff and Services: Free shipping, free returns, no minimums. $10 to spend for joining Nordstrom Rewards.
- Senior Discounts: None found.
- Other Deals and Discounts: Generally you shouldn't expect much in the way of deals when you shop Nordstrom. "Sale" tab on main webpage leads to a handful

of offers. A moderate number of deals (21) were available on the RetailMeNot deal portal.

Ross Stores www.rossstores.com

- Free Stuff and Services: None found.
- Senior Discounts: Discount day—10 percent off on Tuesdays for 55+.
- Other Deals and Discounts: Entire store is a "discounted deal" so no additional deals available through website. E-mail newsletter advises on incoming new products. No deals on RetailMeNot deal portal, either. At least one fake offer through Facebook was reported recently—given their deal policy, it was easy to spot!

Safeway www.safeway.com

- Free Stuff and Services: None found.
- Senior Discounts: None found.
- Other Deals and Discounts: Plenty of deals on the main page and through "Weekly Ad" and "Deals" tiles. Not much portal activity—only nine deals.

Sears Holdings (includes Kmart) www.sears.com

- Free Stuff and Services: Free shipping on "mailable" items; some exclusions apply.
- Senior Discounts: Occasional senior day sales.
- Other Deals and Discounts: Lots of deals on the main page and in "Coupons" and "Local Ad" tabs. Plenty of offers available through deal portals—50 for Sears, 50 for Kmart (in most cases, the same offer)

Target www.target.com

- Free Stuff and Services: Free shipping on orders more than $25.
- Senior Discounts: Recently implemented 10 percent discount for age 60+ to "anyone who self identifies"

and "which cashiers [will] trust each patron to disclose truthfully."

- Other Deals and Discounts: Veteran's Advantage members save 10 percent on a $70 purchase. Main web page is full of discounts, and there is a "Weekly Ad" tab. Target is pretty active in deal portals, with 44 deals when I took the snapshot.

TJX (TJMaxx) www.tjmaxx.com

- Free Stuff and Services: Free shipping for joining the e-mail list or for a $35 purchase.
- Senior Discounts: Senior discount day—Monday, 10 percent off for those 55+.
- Other Deals and Discounts: Very few deals on the website, but moderately active on the portal front with thirty-four deals.

Toys R Us www.toysrus.com

- Free Stuff and Services: Free shipping on orders of $19 or more.
- Senior Discounts: None found.
- Other Deals and Discounts: Deals and offers on main page and through e-mails. Somewhat active on deal portals— with 18 offers.

Trader Joe's www.traderjoes.com

- Free Stuff and Services: Plenty of food information, recipes, and dietary and scientific facts. "Gluten-free" food is far easier to find in a search than "free" food.
- Senior Discounts: None found.
- Other Deals and Discounts: Assumption is that they have the best deals already, so no deals on main webpage. Not active through portals either—only one portal "deal" and it was for a free "Fearless Flyer" deal newsletter—not a very big deal at all!

Walgreens (and Duane Reade) www.walgreens.com

- Free Stuff and Services: Free one to three day shipping on orders more than $30.
- Senior Discounts: Seniors day—15 to 20 percent, online only, one set day a month, 55 and over or AARP members, requires membership to their Balance Rewards program. (See www.walgreens.com/topic/promotion/seniorday.jsp.)
- Other Deals and Discounts: Military discount offered but varies; you'll have to ask. Dozens of deals on main page, "Weekly Ad & Coupons" tab. Active in deal portals—50 deals.

Walmart www.walmart.com

- Free Stuff and Services: There is anecdotal evidence—and a link on the main page—to sign up for regular free samples. But following this link got me nowhere on this cluttered site.
- Senior Discounts: There's some anecdotal evidence of senior discounts given in some stores, but I'm saying, "None found."
- Other Deals and Discounts: Dozens of deals on the main page organized by product category. "Clear-Out" tile front and center on the main page with dozens more items. Moderately active in deal portals— with 45 deals.

Whole Foods Market www.wholefoodsmarket.com

- Free Stuff and Services: Search for "whole foods market free"—and you get a lot of entries for "gluten free"! There are also a lot of recipes, nutrition advisories, and general facts about the foods and vitamins typically sold at Whole Foods.
- Senior Discounts: There is a senior day—but alas, no discount. Seniors instead are given free refreshments and

samples and learn more about healthy alternatives—for only an hour! (See www.wholefoodsmarket.com/store/event/senior-day.)

- Other Deals and Discounts: Not surprisingly, for this "premium" food store, there aren't a lot of deals on their website until you reach an invite to download an app for digital coupons (which I didn't do). At the bottom of the lengthy page is a "Coupons" link, which operates by location. Once you find it, there are a few dozen pretty good deals. Clearly they want you to do this through the app and your smartphone. Whole Foods isn't very active in deal portals with only two deals at present.

Index

M

N

About the Author

Peter Sander (Granite Bay, CA) is an author, researcher, and consultant in the fields of personal finance, business, and location reference. Many of his 49 books specialize in finding value in personal finances (*The Pocket Idiot's Guide to Living on a Budget, 573 Ways to Save Money*); investments (the *100 Best Stocks to Buy* series, *Value Investing for Dummies*); general business (*Negotiating 101*) and places to live (the *Cities Ranked & Rated* series). Other titles include *What Would Steve Jobs Do?, 101 Things Everyone Should Know About Economics,* and *The 25 Habits of Highly Successful Investors.* He has an MBA from Indiana University and has completed Certified Financial Planner (CFP®) education and examination requirements.